MYSTERIES
of SILVER PEAK

Dear Reader,

Much like Sadie, I like to attend estate auctions. The items on sale tell a story about the previous owner's life, and each antique often has its own story too. Back in the late seventies, one of my best finds at an estate auction was an LP of the musical soundtrack *Seven Brides for Seven Brothers*. I played that record over and over, enjoying every song on the album.

The way we play music has changed since then but, as the saying goes, everything old is new again. My daughter recently asked for a record player for her birthday and now has fun playing vinyl records. That inspired me to write about a special record player that kicks off the story in *The Counterfeit Caper*. Strange events from the past lead Sadie into dangerous territory and to an uncertain future.

So settle in for another fun mystery in the quaint town of Silver Peak and enjoy spending time with Sadie and her friends.

Blessings,
Kristin Eckhardt
writing as Carole Jefferson

Mysteries of Silver Peak

MYSTERIES
of SILVER PEAK

The Counterfeit Caper

CAROLE JEFFERSON

Guideposts
New York

Mysteries of Silver Peak is a trademark of Guideposts.

Published by Guideposts Books & Inspirational Media
110 William Street
New York, New York 10038
Guideposts.org

Acknowledgments

Every attempt has been made to credit the sources of copyrighted material used in this book. If any such acknowledgment has been inadvertently omitted or miscredited, receipt of such information would be appreciated.

Scripture quotations are taken from *The Holy Bible, New International Version*. Copyright © 1973, 1978, 1984, 2011 by Biblica, Inc. Used by permission of Zondervan. All rights reserved worldwide. www.zondervan.com

Cover and interior design by Müllerhaus
Cover art by Greg Copeland represented by Deborah Wolfe, Ltd.
Typeset by Aptara, Inc.

Printed and bound in the United States of America
10 9 8 7 6 5 4

The Counterfeit Caper

Prologue

October 19, 1902

Silver Peak, Colorado

DEAR DIARY,

Mother worries that I shall never leave my room and believes all my tears will make me ill. The doctor came yesterday to dose me with laudanum. I heard him speaking in whispers to Mother and Father. They have even placed straw upon the street outside the house to quiet the carriages that go by. As if we are a family in mourning.

Only no one has died.

Mother does not know that my tears dried up days ago. I shall not cry again for that man. My anger has burned away all the love I once held in my heart for him.

Now all I want is vengeance.

So I plan. And I wait. And I stay in my room to avoid the looks of pity that are sure to be directed my way.

But woe to those who dare pity me. I am to be feared. I may be a woman scorned, but I am not weak. And I shall do whatever is necessary to turn his life to ashes.

1

———

"Sadie, you've hardly touched a bite. Are you all right?"

Sadie looked up from her plate to see Cecile Daly staring at her from across the table. Cecile's bright blue eyes, pixie blonde hair, and petite figure toned by a daily jog, made her appear much younger than her sixty years.

"Oh, I'm fine," Sadie replied with a smile, realizing she'd been pushing the creamed peas around on her plate without actually eating them. And they were delicious creamed peas too. Everything on the menu at the Drover Dell Diner was delicious, and all made from scratch.

"I think she's nervous about the auction this afternoon," Roz confided, giving both Cecile and Alfred Daly a smile. "She couldn't talk about anything else during the drive from Silver Peak."

"Are you hoping to buy something in particular?" Cecile asked Sadie.

"Well, there are several things listed on the auction bill that caught my attention," Sadie said, "but I need to see them before I know if they're worth bidding on." She didn't mention the item that had her stomach tied up in knots, afraid she might jinx herself if she spoke of it.

Sadie pushed up the sleeves of her coral-hued crew-neck sweater, feeling a little warm on this cool September day. "I've been to hundreds of auctions in my life, but I'll admit this one has given me a small case of the jitters. It's silly, I know."

"Nothing silly about it," Alfred said, reaching up to straighten his blue bow tie. He wore a dark gray suit that provided a sharp contrast to his thick, wavy white hair. "The Ferris family estate auction has had people talking for months. I've heard there are antique dealers coming in from all over the state."

"That's true." Sadie plucked the white linen napkin from her lap and placed it next to her plate, giving up on the creamed peas, meat loaf, and mashed potatoes she'd ordered for lunch. "The auction sheet was over ten pages long, and that's not including the smaller items for sale."

Cecile speared a small golden beet from the roasted beet salad in front of her. "And they can sell that much in one afternoon?"

"No," Sadie replied, "most of the larger items from the estate and carriage house were slated to go up for sale this morning, like the old horse-drawn sleigh and carriages, the vintage gazebos, the cars, and all of the other outside items the Ferris family owned." She glanced down at her watch, just to be certain their lunch didn't go too long. "This afternoon, they'll be selling the antiques and collectibles from the inside of the Ferris mansion."

Roz eagerly rubbed her hands together, her bangle bracelets jangling on her wrists. "I just can't wait to see it all! Sadie tells me some of the items were made all the way back in the seventeenth century."

Alfred nodded. "That's right. And most of them will go for a pretty penny, I'm sure."

"And that's why I'm nervous," Sadie confided with a small chuckle. "And probably not very good company today either."

"Nonsense," Alfred countered, peering at her through his wire-rimmed glasses. Amusement gleamed in his gentle gray eyes. "You and Roz are both wonderful company. Cecile and I were thrilled when you called and asked us to join you for lunch."

"We certainly were," Cecile chimed. "In fact, we need to do this more often."

"I agree," Sadie said as the waitress stopped by to refill their coffee cups.

The Drover Dell was a small diner located in the heart of downtown Breckenridge and had been in business for over forty years. The diner's daily specials, listed on a large chalkboard in the front window, always included their popular bison burgers and home-cut, sweet potato fries. Alfred and Cecile had introduced the diner to Sadie and her late husband, T.R., over two decades ago, and the four of them had enjoyed many a lively meal there.

Today was no different, as Cecile talked about her plans to start taking French lessons in anticipation of a trip to Paris that she hoped to take with Alfred. "If he ever retires," Cecile said, giving her husband a playful wink.

"Retire?" Alfred said, feigning horror at the word. "I'm much too young for that. I've got another fifteen or twenty years left in me before that happens."

"Then I may have to go to Paris without you," Cecile teased, before their conversation turned to their families and mutual acquaintances.

Sadie told them about her grandson, Theo, and his upcoming college tour. "It's still preliminary, since Theo is only a junior, but he wants to get a jump on things. And to Alice, it's a great excuse to spend a big chunk of one-on-one time with Theo before he's out of the house. Which means I get to enjoy Sara spending the next two weeks with me."

"How fun!" Cecile exclaimed. "How old is she now? Fourteen?"

"That's right," Sadie replied with a wistful sigh. "She and Theo have grown up so fast." Despite her wish that her grandchildren were still young enough to rock to sleep at night, Sadie thanked God for them every day, and for her daughter, Alice. All three of them were such a blessing in her life.

Roz and the Dalys were a blessing too, she realized, as she listened to Roz tell Cecile and Alfred about her two sons.

After a few minutes, Alfred turned to Sadie. "So have you planned your strategy for today's auction?"

Sadie chuckled. "The only strategy I have is to bid higher than the next guy, if possible." She tilted her head to one side. "Are you sure you don't have time to drop in at the estate auction?" She knew that, as a professor of American history at Colorado Mining College, Alfred enjoyed antiques and artifacts from the past as much as she did. "Even for a few minutes?"

"I wish I could," he said wistfully. "But I have a meeting at two that I just can't miss."

Cecile said, "The chair of the history department is looking for someone to fill the assistant chair position that just opened up." A proud smile curved her mouth. "I think he's got his eye on Alfred."

Roz's green eyes widened. "My, how exciting for you, Alfred."

He chuckled. "It may sound that way, but as the assistant chair I'll just get most of the work and none of the glory." He turned to his wife. "Along with some late-night meetings, dear."

Cecile reached over to pat his arm, her skin still a lovely, golden tan from the long hours she'd spent in her garden over the summer. "I won't mind. You deserve a promotion after all the time you've given the college."

Roz picked up her coffee cup. "With the recent spate of burglaries in Breckenridge that I've been reading about in the paper, I'm not sure I'd feel safe staying home alone."

"I've heard about them too," Sadie said, turning to Alfred and Cecile. "Have there been any break-ins in your neighborhood?"

Cecile shook her head. "Fortunately for us, the burglar, or burglars, seem to be targeting the high-end houses located on the outskirts of town. The most recent break-in happened at the King of Fakes' house."

Roz blinked. "The king of what?"

"Fakes," Alfred said with a smile. "It's a moniker the man coined himself." He turned to Sadie. "You know who we mean, I'm sure."

Sadie nodded. "Brent Fielder." She smiled at Roz. "He's one of the country's biggest collectors of famous fakes, frauds, and forgeries."

Roz laughed. "I think the three of you are pulling my leg!"

"No, it's true," Cecile said.

"Every word of it." Alfred, a former Eagle Scout, held up his hand in the two-finger Boy Scout salute. "Although, to be fair, Fielder collects many authentic antiques and artifacts too."

Roz didn't look convinced. "But why would someone want to collect fakes?"

"I think the novelty of it is part of the appeal," Sadie mused.

"And it actually can be lucrative too," Alfred added. "There are several stories of fake antiquities fooling experts in the field, and of bringing a huge amount of money from collectors who are none the wiser. But those high-quality fakes are rare, which makes them appealing to a certain segment of collectors. It's usually the folklore behind the fakes that gives them the most value."

"Like the Great Brewster Chair acquired by the Henry Ford Museum back in the seventies," Sadie said in agreement. "The museum paid nine thousand dollars for a chair that was once believed to have belonged to William Brewster, one of the men who established the Massachusetts Bay Colony way back in 1620."

"And it was a fake?" Roz asked.

Sadie nodded. "Turns out it was built in 1969 and designed to fool the experts. The museum still displays it as an example of how authentic a fake antique can appear."

"And they paid nine thousand for that example," Alfred said with a smile. "The Great Brewster Chair is the kind of item that the King of Fakes would love to have for his collection."

Roz looked bemused. "So did the thief steal some of Brent Fielder's fakes or his real collectibles?"

"The police aren't releasing that information," Alfred said with a shrug.

"And it might not matter," Sadie ventured. "Since most of Fielder's fakes have fooled the experts at one time or another in the past, he could pass them off as the real thing."

Alfred leaned back in his chair and steepled his fingers. "The recent Pederson burglary is the one that's got everyone talking at the university. Oliver Pederson lost an original Monet painting valued in the six figures, along with several pieces of his wife's diamond and emerald jewelry."

"I heard the mayor's house was robbed too," Cecile said.

"Oh my," Sadie said, shaking her head. "Do the police have any leads?"

"Maybe." Cecile placed her napkin on her plate. "My cousin works at the police department, and she hinted that they may be closing in on the thief."

"Let's hope it's true," Alfred said, then turned to Sadie. "And speaking of mayors, how is Edwin?"

"He's fine," she said with a smile. "He seems to thrive in his duties as Silver Peak's mayor. I'm so proud of him."

"You should be," Roz told her. "He's doing a great job."

When the waitress approached their table to gather some of the empty plates, Sadie glanced at her watch again. "Oh, Roz, we need to scoot if we don't want the afternoon session to start without us."

Roz rose from the table. "Well, it looks like we're going to eat and run." Then she looked at Sadie's plate. "Do you want a doggie bag to take with you?"

Sadie considered it for a moment, given the large amount of food still left on her plate, then she shook her head. "No, I don't want the food sitting in my car all afternoon."

"I'll take it," Alfred said with a smile. "There's nothing better than a cold meat-loaf sandwich for a midnight snack."

"Oh, Alfred," Cecile said, trying to stifle her laughter.

Sadie laughed too. "Yes, please, do take it, Alfred. That way it won't go to waste."

Alfred asked the waitress for a doggie bag while Sadie and Roz headed to the cash register to settle up their bill.

A few minutes later, the four of them stood on the brick sidewalk outside the diner. "Good luck at the auction," Cecile told Sadie, reaching out to give her a hug. "Let us know how it goes."

"I will," Sadie promised, bidding farewell to Alfred as Roz hugged Cecile.

Then they were on their way.

Three hours later, Sadie and Roz sat among the crowd of bidders and onlookers at the Ferris estate auction.

"Are you still nervous?" Roz asked, wearing the pair of emerald-green cat-eye glasses she'd fished out of her purse on the way over.

"No, but I am starving," Sadie said wryly, wishing she'd eaten more of her lunch. "Who knew the auction would take this long?"

Roz grinned. "The food truck is selling soft pretzels with cheese. That might hit the spot."

"Don't tempt me," Sadie replied. She'd been trying to ignore that food truck, with all of its sweet and savory temptations, since they'd arrived at the estate auction three hours ago.

They'd already been here much longer than she'd expected. She'd hoped to spend part of the afternoon getting ready for Sara's visit tomorrow, but at this rate, she'd be lucky to be home by dusk.

Undeterred, Sadie sat up and squared her shoulders, not planning to leave the auction until the item that had brought her to Breckenridge came up for sale. She looked around the large auditorium, her bidding card clasped in her right hand.

To her dismay, the Ferris estate auction had caught the attention of several antique buyers in the area, along with some of the long-distance buyers that Alfred had mentioned.

The Ferris family had settled in Breckenridge in the late 1800s and been well known around the state for their philanthropy.

Sadie and her late husband, T.R., had attended a large charity gala at the Ferris mansion several years before, and Sadie had marveled at the huge array of antiques and collectibles that had filled the home.

When ninety-eight-year-old Eulalie Ferris passed away a few months ago, Sadie had been surprised to learn that her heirs planned to sell off all the household contents, including the antiques. As with many auctions, there were some additional consignment items added from private owners, to draw even more interest in the sale.

But of all the lavish antiques and collectibles on the auction bill, Sadie had her heart set on only one of them. It was the antique phonograph that she'd seen at the Ferris gala all those years ago. A Victor Orthophonic Credenza model—the rare one with a tooled Moroccan leather front, it was an exact match for the phonograph once owned by her grandparents. The Orthophonic models were a huge technological leap over the old Victrolas, with fuller, richer sound that was capable of reproducing the new electric recordings that came with the talking picture era. Grandpa had taught her to dance to the 78 rpm records played on that phonograph. She'd sung hymns with her grandmother with music from the phonograph. She'd even enjoyed her first dance with Edwin to the 1960 hit song "This Magic Moment" played on that phonograph.

She'd never seen another one like it since the Ferris gala and had even offered to buy it from Eulalie at the time. Eulalie had politely declined, but now Sadie had her chance. She couldn't ever remember being this nervous and excited at an auction before, and she took a deep breath to calm herself.

"Take another breath," Roz said with a smile, reaching out to gently pat her arm. "You've got this."

"I hope so, but you never know. There are a lot of dealers here today. I just wish it wasn't taking so long."

"I know what you mean." Roz leaned back in her chair. "We've been here long enough that I've actually decided to bid on something."

Sadie appreciated the fact that Roz enjoyed attending antique auctions with her, although she rarely bid on anything. "What is it?"

"One of the mystery boxes," Roz said with a smile. "You know how much I love surprises, and I should find at least one thing I like inside one of those large boxes." She tucked a strand of gray hair behind her ear, the motion causing a melodic tinkle of the gold bangle bracelets adorning her right forearm. More than one antique buyer had approached Roz today to comment on her vintage butter-yellow peasant blouse and pinstriped blue-and-yellow maxiskirt. Roz had soaked up the compliments and couldn't wait to go home and tell Roscoe, since he'd given her the outfit for her birthday.

Sadie chuckled. "You know you're taking a risk, right? They put stuff in those mystery boxes that they believe no one will bid on."

"Oh, I know that," Roz said breezily. "But those mystery boxes don't usually cost too much, do they? I've already decided I won't pay more than twenty dollars."

"That sounds about right for what they're worth." Sadie's gaze moved to the auctioneer at the front of the auditorium. Marvin Burton was one half of the partnership of Burton & Best Auction Services. Marv Burton and Leo Best had been in business together for over twenty years and were both excellent auctioneers. Marv's wife, Starla, assisted at every auction, along with their adult daughter Lisa, who had joined the business a few years ago.

"Item number one hundred fourteen is a Swiss clock, circa 1910, with gold overlay and hand-carved mahogany details," Marv announced to the crowd. "Let's start the bidding at two hundred dollars."

The Victor Orthophonic Credenza model phonograph, the top of the Victor line and built in the late 1920s, was item number 116 in the program, and Sadie could see it lined up on the platform behind the auctioneer. She'd had a chance to examine it before the auction began and was thrilled to see the Moroccan-leather-front cabinet and spring motor were still in excellent condition. Starla had even cranked the machine to play a 78 rpm record.

Smooth, rich music had emerged from the open doors of the large cabinet, filling the auditorium with Beethoven's "Ode to Joy."

While Sadie appreciated the demonstration, she feared it may have drawn even more interest from potential buyers.

As she watched the bidding for item number 114, her heart began to beat a little faster. Despite her impatience, there was something about the sound of an auctioneer's rhythmic patter and the enthusiasm of the bidders around her that lent a wonderful excitement to the air. She'd learned a long time ago that it was easy to get too caught up in that excitement and overbid for an item. That's why she already had a top bid of two thousand dollars in mind for the phonograph and had made a promise to herself to go no higher.

"Sold!" Marv shouted with a sharp rap of his gavel against the wood podium. "The Swiss clock goes to bidder number five hundred seventy-one, with a winning bid of six hundred and thirty dollars."

A spatter of polite applause echoed in the auditorium as Marv's assistant, Lisa, picked up a plain cardboard box about the size of an electric roaster oven and carried it to the empty display table next to Marv.

Marv grinned as he laid one beefy palm on top of the box lid. The mystery boxes had each been sealed shut with tape to keep the curious from taking a peek inside. "And here's item number one hundred fifteen. This is our first mystery box of the day, ladies and gentlemen. The first of four."

Roz sat up straight in her chair. "*Ooh*, this could be it."

Sadie smiled. "What are you hoping to find in there?"

"Oh, I don't know," Roz said, one hand clasping her bidding card. "Some vintage jewelry would be nice. Or books or some milk glass dishes or vases. I could find anything in there. That's what makes it so fun!"

Sadie laughed. "Let's just hope it's not some old burlap feed sacks. That happened to me once with a mystery box, remember?"

"I sure do," Roz said, laughing with her. "But you managed to make some cute place mats out of them. As I recall, you sold enough of those place mats to recoup the money you spent on the box."

"Plus a little extra," Sadie said with a nod. "That's called making lemonade out of lemons. Or bucks out of burlap, as the case may be."

Sadie heard Roz chuckle as they both turned their attention toward the auctioneer.

"Time for a little mystery, ladies and gentlemen," Marv announced. "I've heard that our first mystery box contains some delightful items." He grinned, revealing a silver crown around one front tooth. "Let's start with ten dollars, folks."

Sadie saw a man in the front row raise his hand in the air. "Ten!"

Marv nodded in the man's direction to acknowledge the bid and then continued his fast-paced chant. "Ten-dollar bid by the gentleman up front. Now eleven, now eleven, will ya give me eleven?"

Roz's hand shot up. "Eleven!"

"Eleven is bid by the pretty lady," the auctioneer said. "Now fifteen, now fifteen, will ya give me fifteen?"

"Twenty!" a man shouted from the back.

"Oh, I hate that," Roz whispered to her. "Why do they have to jump so high?"

"Probably hoping to scare off other bidders," Sadie said.

"I've got twenty," the auctioneer said, "now twenty-one, now twenty-one, for this fine mystery box. Will ya give me twenty-one!"

"Twenty-one," called out the man from the front row.

The auctioneer pointed at him. "We've got twenty-one." His gaze moved to Roz. "Twenty-two? Will ya give me twenty-two?"

"Twenty-two," Roz shouted, half-standing up from her chair. Then she turned to smile at Sadie. "Two can play at that game."

"Pretty lady bids twenty-two," Marv said. "Now twenty-three, now twenty-three..."

"Twenty was your high bid," Sadie reminded her, getting caught up in the excitement herself. "And there are three more mystery boxes."

"I know." Roz flashed another smile. "But I really want this one. I just have a good feeling about it."

The man in the front row raised his arm in the air. "Twenty-three."

"Oh no," Roz breathed, then bit her bottom lip.

"I've got twenty-three. Now give me twenty-four, now twenty-four." Marv paused for a moment, his keen-eyed gaze scanning the room. "Last chance for twenty-four."

Sadie stood up and cried, "Twenty-four!"

Roz turned to gape at her. "What are you doing?"

"*Sh*," she said with a smile, "I have to pay attention."

"Twenty-four," Marv announced, looking once more around the room. After a long pause, he said, "Going once...going twice. Sold!"

Marv's gavel struck the podium.

"You won!" Sadie reached over to give Roz a hug. "We don't know what you won, but you won!"

"You mean *you* won," Roz said with a grin.

"No, you won," Sadie insisted. "Remember the four dollars I borrowed from you the other day when we had breakfast at Flap Jack's? Well, consider yourself repaid."

Roz laughed. "Well, then I guess I did win." She raised both arms in the air, her gold bracelets jangling at the movement. "Woo-hoo! I can't wait to see what's inside my box."

"We'll find out soon." Sadie shifted in her chair. "The phonograph is up next. We can leave after it sells."

A wave of excited murmurs swept through the crowd as two men carefully hoisted the Victor Orthophonic Credenza model and carried it to the table near the podium. As the gorgeous Moroccan leather trim shone under the bright auditorium lights, the tune of "This Magic Moment" began to play in Sadie's head.

She shook it off, needing her full concentration for the bidding ahead. She knew from experience that one of the most important parts of the bidding process was assessing your competition.

Sadie took a slow, deep breath, telling herself not to get her hopes up too high. But she could already picture the phonograph in her shop and even had a spot picked out for it. Her grandparents' phonograph had been willed away long ago, but Sadie still had all of their 78 rpm records.

"Are you ready?" Roz whispered to her.

"I think so," Sadie said, waiting for the bidding to begin.

Marv gave the phonograph a long, appreciative look before turning his attention to the audience. "Ladies and gentlemen, item number one hundred sixteen is truly special. I've been in this business a long time, and I can honestly say that this is one of the finest Victor Orthophonic Credenza model phonographs I've ever come across. This was the top o' the line, folks. The crème de la crème."

"It is lovely," Roz murmured.

"It was purchased by the Ferris family around 1928," Marv continued, "and remained in the family through all these years. It's been well-maintained, and as many of you heard earlier, the sound quality is amazing."

"Oh, Sadie," Roz said, holding out her hand to show her fingers trembling, "now I'm nervous too!"

"All right, everybody," Marv called out to the crowd, "let's start the bidding!"

2

SADIE HELD HER BREATH AS THE BIDDING ON THE PHONOGRAPH began.

"Do I hear five hundred dollars?" Marv cried. "Who will give me five hundred?"

"Five hundred," shouted a man several rows behind Sadie.

"Now six," Marv said, getting into his cadence. "Will ya give me six hundred for this amazing piece of musical history?"

"Six hundred," said a woman near the front.

From that point, the bidding began moving at a rapid pace and Sadie counted six different bidders vying for the phonograph before she was able to make a bid of her own.

"Twelve hundred," Sadie called out, raising her bidding card in the air.

"Sadie bids twelve," Marv said with a nod of recognition in her direction. "Now thirteen..."

"Thirteen," Herbert Wynot cried out from the front row. Sadie had known Herbert for years and they'd bid against each other countless times. He owned an antique store in Breckenridge and had a good eye for quality pieces, although he often paid more than they were worth.

"Fourteen hundred," Sadie countered, determined not to let him win this time.

"Fifteen!" Herbert waved his card in the air.

The auctioneer kept up with the fast pace, his eyes alight with enthusiasm. "Now fifteen, will ya give me sixteen?"

"Sixteen," shouted the man in the back.

Sadie's hand shot into the air. "Seventeen."

"Eighteen," Herbert countered.

The bidding was getting dangerously close to Sadie's top number of two thousand dollars. "Nineteen," she called out.

"Now nineteen," the auctioneer said, looking toward Herbert.

"Two thousand dollars," Herbert said calmly, as if he could sit there and bid all day.

Sadie's stomach began to sink. Maybe if she just bid one more time. "Twenty-one hundred," she said, certain she could still make a profit on the phonograph if she chose to sell it. She could feel Roz's gaze on her but kept her focus on the auctioneer.

"Now give me twenty-two hundred," Marvin said to the crowd. "Do I hear twenty-two?"

For a moment, Herbert just sat there. Roz reached over and gave Sadie's hand an encouraging squeeze.

"Twenty-two?" Marv said, looking around the auditorium. "Do I hear twenty-two?"

Sadie closed her eyes, hope welling within her as she waited for the sound of the gavel to hit the podium. More than anything, she wanted the auctioneer to yell the word *Sold!* and point in her direction.

"I bid twenty-two hundred," Herbert suddenly called out.

The sound of his voice made Sadie's stomach drop to her toes. For one long moment, she considered bidding twenty-three hundred. After all, Herbert's hesitation before that last bid might be a sign that he'd reached his limit too.

But she knew better.

After bidding against him for years, Sadie had learned Herbert rarely quit after bidding that high. He often let the competition of the bidding carry him away—something Sadie had promised herself not to do today.

The auctioneer looked in Sadie's direction. "Now twenty-three. Do I hear twenty-three?"

She slowly shook her head, her lips pressed firmly together to keep from blurting out another bid.

She'd lost the phonograph.

"Oh, Sadie," Roz said with a low groan.

"I know," she said, her voice tight. She steeled herself for the sight of watching Herbert walk away with her Victor Orthophonic.

"Twenty-two hundred going once. Going twice...," Marv said, his gavel poised in the air.

Out of the corner of her eye, Sadie could see Herbert sitting up straight in his chair, a satisfied smile curving his mouth.

"Twenty-three hundred," said a man's voice behind her.

She glanced over her shoulder at the man who had just outbid Herbert. He looked about forty years old and wore a black suit with a silver-gray tie. His dark hair and aristocratic face reminded her a little of Cary Grant. She'd never seen him before, but the auction had brought antique dealers from the far corners of the state.

"Twenty-four hundred," Herbert blurted out, directing a glare in the new bidder's direction.

"Twenty-five hundred," said the Cary Grant look-alike.

The auctioneer looked over at Herbert. "Now twenty-six?"

Herbert nodded.

The auctioneer's gaze moved to Herbert's new nemesis. "Now twenty-seven. Will ya give me twenty-seven?"

"Twenty-seven," the man said without hesitation.

"Now twenty-eight," the auctioneer said to Herbert.

After a long hesitation, Herbert grimly shook his head.

"Twenty-seven hundred once," the auctioneer warned. "Twenty-seven hundred twice." Marvin paused for a moment, the gavel poised in his hand. Then he grinned and slammed the gavel down on the podium. "Sold!"

The audience burst into applause, showing their appreciation for the robust bidding. Sadie applauded along with them, hoping the winning bidder would appreciate the treasure he'd just won. She turned around to congratulate him but was surprised to see that he was already gone.

Sadie decided to follow his example. "Are you ready to go?" she asked Roz, suddenly eager to get back home to Silver Peak.

"Wait," Roz said, staring at the auction table. "Is that a Steiff?"

Sadie followed her gaze and watched as Marv picked up a teddy bear. A very old teddy bear. "It sure looks like it."

Opening her auction catalog, Sadie once more looked over the list of items for sale. "But I've read through this catalog twice and didn't see a Steiff bear listed."

"Neither did I," Roz said, picking up her blue leather fringe bag and slinging it over her shoulder. "Okay, I'm ready if you are."

They both stood up as Marv began to speak to the crowd.

"Ladies and gentleman, we have a nice surprise here today. It's a last-minute addition to our auction and one I simply couldn't refuse." Marv's voice lowered a notch and took on an almost reverent tone. "This is a 1907 Steiff teddy bear, and it appears to be in very good condition..."

"Wait," Sadie said, grabbing Roz's arm. "It really is a Steiff!"

"See, you've taught me well," Roz said with a smile.

"Well, we can't leave now," Sadie said, suddenly buoyed by this unexpected development. There were some antiques and collectibles that Sadie just couldn't pass by and Steiff teddy bears were among them. She owned one herself—an adorable 1910 brown teddy bear that had belonged to her great-grandmother and had been passed down through the generations. Someday, she planned to give it to her granddaughter, Sara, who had often played with it at Sadie's house.

"As you know," Marv continued, "most of the items here today are from the estate of Eulalie Ferris, but on occasion we will include other unique items on consignment. This is one such item, and I'd like to get the bidding started at five hundred dollars."

Sadie glanced over at Herbert, but he sat stiffly in his chair, not even looking at the new item up for bid. No doubt he was still miffed about losing the phonograph. That meant less competition for the teddy bear.

Still, the fact that the Steiff bear was a last-minute addition meant that she didn't have the information she needed to make a solid estimate. Still, however, she'd been in the business long enough to know a good quality Steiff when she saw one.

The teddy bear up for bid now looked like one of the best she'd ever seen.

Sadie did a quick calculation in her head and then listened for the most recent bid. She raised her card in the air and shouted, "Nine hundred."

"Nine hundred," Marv said, nodding toward her. "Now a thousand, do I hear a thousand?"

A woman near the front raised her hand. "One thousand."

"Twelve hundred," Sadie said before the auctioneer could ask for the next bid. From the corner of her eye, she saw Herbert get up from his chair and walk out of the auditorium.

"Now thirteen hundred?" the auctioneer said.

The woman nodded. "Thirteen."

"Now fourteen hundred," Marv said, his gaze on Sadie.

Sadie raised her hand. "Fourteen hundred."

"Now fifteen?" the auctioneer said to the woman.

The woman in the front row hesitated, then shook her head.

Sadie's heart began to pound as she waited for someone else to bid.

"Now fifteen," the auctioneer said, scanning the crowd. "Will ya give me fifteen hundred? Now fifteen?"

Sadie watched the auctioneer's fingers wrap around the gavel's handle. She held her breath and waited, hoping to hear the bang.

"All right, then," Marv said, his gavel poised in the air. "Going once for fourteen hundred dollars. Going twice..."

Sadie held her breath, her heart racing now.

"Sold!" Marv shouted, pounding his gavel down on the podium with a resounding *smack*.

The sound was music to Sadie's ears.

"You got it!" Roz exclaimed, turning toward her.

"I did!" Sadie said, reaching over to give her a quick hug. "I really did!" She'd been ready to bid up to two thousand dollars for the teddy bear, so it had been a real steal. "I can't wait to get my hands on it."

"Oh, we're going to have such a fun ride home," Roz said cheerfully as they rose to their feet and made their way to the cashier's table. "We can get a closer look at your teddy bear and dig into my mystery box. I can't wait to see what we find."

Neither could Sadie. Something told her that their fun was just beginning.

The two cashier tables made the lines move fairly quickly. The first was manned by Lisa Burton and designated for items that had sold for under one thousand dollars. Starla Burton stood behind the second table, which had been designated for items sold for one thousand dollars and over.

Sadie and Roz headed to Lisa's table first. Since Sadie had actually won the bid for the mystery box, they'd need her bidding card to pick it up. Despite the number of people at the auction, soon they were at the front.

Roz handed Sadie a twenty-dollar bill. "Here's my portion."

"And here's mine," Sadie said, adding four one-dollar bills to the twenty and giving the cash to Lisa.

A moment later, Lisa retrieved the mystery box marked as item 115 and set it on the table in front of her. "Well, that's strange," Lisa said, fingering the loose tape that had been used to seal the box lid. "It looks like some of the security tape came off."

"That's all right," Roz said with a a wave of her hand. "It won't stay closed for long." Then she picked up the mystery box in her arms. "Wow, it's heavier than I expected." She smiled over at Sadie. "I hope that's a good sign."

"Me too."

Roz turned toward the exit doors. "If you don't mind, I'll just meet you at the car."

"I don't mind at all." Sadie handed Roz the keys to her Tahoe. "I shouldn't be too much longer."

"Take your time," Roz said over her shoulder as she headed for the door.

Sadie walked over to the other cashier's table, thrilled to see it was momentarily open. Starla sat behind it, typing on a laptop in front of her.

Starla looked up from the monitor and smiled. "Well, hello, Sadie! I'm happy to see you here today. Did you get what you came for?"

"No, but I'm leaving with something special." She handed her bidding card to Starla and then watched her input the number into the computer.

"The Steiff teddy bear," Starla said, her brown eyes widening as she stared at the computer screen. "Oh my, you got it for a good price too."

"I sure did. And I'd love to know who owned it." Sadie always liked to learn the history behind her antiques. The stories often intrigued her and gave a life to the items that found their way into her shop or home.

"And I wish I could tell you," Starla said with a sigh, "but the seller wished to remain anonymous."

"Really?" Sadie knew some sellers liked their anonymity, but in her experience it wasn't the norm. "Do you know why?"

Starla shrugged as she handed an invoice to Sadie. "I'm afraid not. The teddy bear just arrived this morning, and Marvin was so impressed with it that he decided to add it to the auction at the last minute. I'll bet you were excited to see it come up for bid."

"I sure was." Sadie wrote out a check for fourteen hundred dollars while Starla left to retrieve the teddy bear.

Marvin's deep voice carried through the loudspeakers as the auction continued at a brisk pace. She assumed that his partner, Leo Best, would be showing up soon to relieve him and give his voice a rest.

"Here we go," Starla said, returning with a white paper bag. She handed it over to Sadie. "One Steiff teddy bear."

"Thank you so much." Sadie grabbed the paper bag by its handles and then stepped aside, making room for the next person in line. Despite the crowded auditorium, Sadie couldn't wait a moment longer. She reached inside the paper bag and carefully pulled out the teddy bear.

It was wrapped in a plastic bag specially made for protecting textiles. Sadie gazed at the teddy bear through the clear plastic. It looked even better close-up than it had from afar. The mohair coat was in good condition, and it had the trademark button in one ear that displayed the year the bear was made. Her fingers itched to take the teddy bear out of the plastic for an even closer inspection, but she didn't want to keep Roz waiting.

She turned around to head toward the door and almost ran into Herbert.

"Good afternoon, Sadie," he said with a polite smile. "How are you?"

"Just fine, Herbert. How are you?"

"I'm a bit peeved, if you want to know the truth." He brushed a hand over his carefully combed gray hair. He stood only a couple of inches taller than Sadie and liked to dress in three-piece suits. Today he wore a green-and-blue herringbone suit with a blue vest and tie.

"That Orthophonic Credenza was the sole reason I attended this auction," Herbert continued. "Then some interloper makes a ridiculous overbid." He sniffed. "I guess that's the way it goes in our business, but we don't have to like it."

"There are still quite a few items left in the auction," she told him, knowing all too well how it felt to lose the phonograph. "Perhaps you can still find a good deal."

"No, I'm done," he said decisively. "You know me. I'm not an impulse buyer." He glanced down at the bag in her hand. "How's the teddy bear?"

"It looks great," she said. "But I'll know more once I'm home and get a good look at it."

He smiled. "That's the best part, isn't it?"

She nodded, feeling a camaraderie with Herbert even though they were often competitors. "It sure is."

"Too bad this will probably be the last Burton & Best auction we attend."

Her brow furrowed. "What do you mean?"

"Haven't you heard?" He took a step closer to her and lowered his voice. "Leo is suing Marvin. Says he's been skimming money from the business."

"Oh no," Sadie murmured, not wanting to believe it. But Herbert had always kept his ear close to the antique auction business, so she sensed it was true.

"Oh yes," Herbert countered. "Apparently, there was a big blowout at their last auction in Colorado Springs. Leo called Marv a cheat loud enough for half the people in the place to hear him. Then he stormed off."

"So that must be why Leo's not here today," Sadie mused.

Herbert nodded. "He's probably in a meeting with his lawyer."

Sadie hated to hear about the discord between Marvin and Leo. They'd been together a long time and built a business with a solid reputation.

"Well, I won't keep you," Herbert said with a nod. "Have a nice day, Sadie."

"You too," she said before turning toward the door.

When Sadie arrived at the parking lot, she found Roz waiting for her by the red Tahoe with two soft pretzels smothered in melted cheddar cheese.

"What did you do?" Sadie asked, her mouth already watering.

Roz grinned. "I thought we might like a little snack for the trip home."

"Great idea," Sadie said as she opened the rear hatch of the Tahoe and placed the teddy bear inside. "Did you look inside your mystery box?"

"Not yet. I don't want to spill cheese on it. As curious as I am to see what's inside, I'll wait until we get back to Silver Peak."

Sadie nodded. "That will give us something to look forward to."

Fifteen minutes later, they were on the highway leaving Breckenridge. Sadie had told Roz about the apparent dispute between Marv and Leo while they'd eaten their pretzels in the parking lot, enjoying every bite of the cheesy treats before heading home.

"That was so good," Roz said, licking cheese off her plastic fork. "You know, Roscoe's been talking about putting in a popcorn machine at the hardware store, but maybe I should talk him into a pretzel maker instead."

"Maybe," Sadie murmured, barely aware of the conversation as she glanced in the rearview mirror.

"Sadie?" Roz said, sitting up in her seat. "What's going on?"

Sadie took a deep breath. "Call me crazy, but I think someone may be following us."

3

ROZ GLANCED OVER HER SHOULDER AT THE BACK WINDOW. "ARE you sure we're being followed?"

"No, I'm not," Sadie said calmly. "But that blue car has been right on our tail ever since we left Breckenridge."

"There's no front license plate," Roz said, taking another look through the back window. "Which means it's either a new car or someone who doesn't want to be identified."

"Yes, I noticed that too." Sadie tried to tell herself she was being ridiculous. Why would anyone want to follow them? "I'll try slowing down and see if they pass us."

"Good idea. It might just be some people new to the area who aren't sure where they're going."

Sadie turned off the cruise control on her Tahoe, letting it slowly decelerate. She glanced in the rearview mirror as her car slowed from fifty miles an hour to forty miles an hour. The car behind her kept the same distance between them, which meant that the driver was slowing down too.

"Okay, this is strange," Roz observed. "Why won't he pass us?"

"Or she," Sadie said. "I can't tell if the driver is a man or a woman through that tinted window, or if anyone else is in the car."

"Maybe it's just someone who's skittish about driving on mountain roads," Roz said, "especially if they're new to the area. It can be a little daunting."

Sadie nodded, remembering how her cousin, Laura Finch, had gotten lost among the curving, high mountain roads when she'd first moved here from Massachusetts. "Maybe."

Sadie's cell phone rang on the console next to her. She glanced down to see her daughter's name pop up on the screen. "It's Alice. Will you answer and tell her I'm driving?"

"Sure," Roz said, picking up Sadie's cell phone to take the call. "Hello, Alice. This is Roz." She smiled over at Sadie. "Your mom's driving right now, so you're stuck talking to me."

Then Sadie had another idea. If she pulled over, would the car behind her pull over too, or just keep going? When there was plenty of room on the road, she slowed down and steered her Tahoe carefully onto the gravel shoulder before placing the gear shift into park.

As Roz chatted with Alice, Sadie's gaze stayed on the rearview mirror. The car behind them slowed for a moment, then accelerated and sped around them. Sadie grabbed Roz's cell phone from the console and quickly snapped a picture as the blue car zoomed in front of them. The mud-splattered license plate made it impossible to see the numbers clearly.

Soon the car was out of sight.

Sadie breathed a sigh of relief. "Okay, I can talk to her now."

"Here's your mom," Roz said before handing over the phone.

"Hi, honey," Sadie said into the phone.

"Hey, Mom," Alice said. "How was the estate auction?"

"Good," Sadie told her. "There was quite a crowd."

"Did you get the phonograph?" Alice asked.

"No, I was outbid. But I did walk away with a very nice Steiff teddy bear."

"Oh, I'm sorry about the phonograph. I know how much you wanted it."

"These things happen," Sadie said, her own disappointment now a dull ache in her heart. "Are you and Theo ready for your big trip?"

"Actually, that's why I'm calling," Alice said. "We're going to try to squeeze in another college visit, which means we'll have to leave for Denver tonight. Do you mind if I drop off Sara tonight instead of tomorrow?"

"Mind?" Sadie said with a smile. "I think that's a great plan."

Alice laughed. "Perfect. Do you know what time you'll be home?"

"We're about fifteen minutes away from the house," Sadie told her. "Are you coming over right away?"

"Yes, we'll meet you there."

"Sounds good. See you soon." Sadie ended the call and then turned to Roz. "Alice and the kids are on their way to the house."

"I heard." Roz grinned. "An extra day with your granddaughter sounds like another early birthday present. It doesn't get better than that."

Sadie's smile widened as she shifted her SUV into gear and pulled back onto the empty highway. "I'll have to think of something special to fix for supper now. Barbecued ribs is one of her favorites, but I'm not sure if I have any barbecue sauce in the pantry."

Roz laughed. "You don't have to fix her favorite dish on her first night."

"That's true. She'll be staying with me long enough to make all her favorites."

"Sounds like you'll be cooking up a storm," Roz said, reaching up to adjust her hearing aid. "And speaking of cooking, that car behind us took off like it was on fire. I guess we finally slowed down enough to make him pass us."

"I snapped a picture with your phone, but now I doubt he was following us. I've probably been watching too many detective movies lately," Sadie said with a smile. "Oh, that reminds me. Could I borrow your *Maltese Falcon* DVD? Sara's never seen it, and I know we'll have a movie night or two while she's here."

"Sure. I'll bring it to your shop next time I come by."

Sadie turned off the mountain road and headed down her long driveway, the small rocks crunching under her tires. A breeze fluttered the green leaves on the tall aspen trees on either side of the driveway.

As they approached the house, Sadie saw Alice's blue Jeep Cherokee already parked there, right next to Roz's car. Alice and the kids were seated on the front porch.

"You beat us home," Sadie called out as she and Roz climbed out of the Tahoe.

"And we brought pizza," Sara announced, holding up a large cardboard pizza box.

Roz chuckled as she and Sadie walked to the front porch. "I guess you don't have to fix supper now."

Alice reached out to give Sadie a warm hug. "There's more than enough pizza for everyone." Then she turned to Roz. "I hope you can stay and eat with us."

"I'd love to," Roz replied. "It's Roscoe's bowling night, so he won't miss me."

Sadie unlocked the front door and led the way inside. "You didn't have to wait on the porch, Alice. You have a house key."

"I know, Mom, but it's so nice out today. Before long we'll have too much snow to sit on your front porch, so I'm going to enjoy it while I can."

"I can't wait for winter to get here," Theo said as they made their way into the kitchen. "That means skiing and snowboarding and snowball fights. Fun times."

Sara set the pizza box down on the table. "Not so fun when I'm the one getting hit by those snowballs. But my aim is getting better, so you'd better watch out."

The kids continued to banter while Sadie retrieved some plates and glasses from the cupboard. Alice made a pitcher of iced tea while Roz helped Sadie set the table.

Then they all sat down to say grace. Sadie treasured this moment with her family and best friend, adding a silent prayer of thanks to God for all of her blessings.

After the final "Amen," Theo sat up in his chair and lunged past his sister to grab the first slice of pizza.

"Hey," Sara protested, picking up a small, roasted mushroom that had fallen from his slice and onto her plate, "that's rude." Then she popped the mushroom into her mouth.

"Sorry, sis," Theo said. "I'm just excited to get going. Dad's going to meet us at the hotel by the Denver airport so we can go over our schedule."

Roz cut a wedge of pizza in half and then placed a thin slice on her plate. "So Cliff is going with you?" she asked Alice, referring to Alice's ex-husband.

"Only on the first leg of the trip," Alice told her. "He went to college at Michigan State and wants to show Theo around the campus himself."

"That's nice," Sadie said. "So you said on the phone that you're planning an extra tour?"

Alice nodded as she dabbed at a spot of tomato sauce on one corner of her mouth. "A tour slot opened up at Northwestern College in Chicago, so we decided to take advantage of it since it's located only a couple of hours' driving distance from the University of Illinois."

They chatted about Theo's upcoming college tours as they ate pizza and finished off the meal with some of Sadie's homemade brownies topped with vanilla ice cream.

"That should hold me until we get to Denver." Theo patted his stomach as they all got up from the table.

"Speaking of Denver," Alice said, glancing at her watch, "we'd better get going if we want to meet your dad on time."

Theo walked over to Sadie and slung a lanky arm around her shoulder. "'Bye, Grandma. I hope Sara doesn't give you too much trouble."

Sara snorted behind him. "Right. Like I'm the troublemaker in this family."

Sadie hugged him, so proud of her tall, handsome grandson. "Have fun on your trip, Theo. I want to hear all about it when you get home."

Alice embraced her daughter in a big hug, and then walked over to hug Sadie. "Thanks again, Mom. If you need anything, call me anytime, day or night."

"Don't worry, dear," Sadie said, giving her daughter a warm squeeze. "Sara and I will get along fine. You just relax and have a good time."

Alice and Theo said their good-byes to Roz, and then Theo gently punched his sister on the upper arm. "Hey, try not to miss me too much, munchkin."

Sara stuck out her tongue at him, but she walked onto the front porch to watch them leave, waving until they reached the end of the long driveway and drove out of sight.

"Oh my," Roz said, placing a hand on her stomach as she and Sadie stood in the open doorway. "I don't think I'll be able to eat for a week. Pizza and a brownie sundae on top of that cheesy pretzel was too much food—even for me!"

Sadie chuckled, feeling a little full herself, although she'd skipped the pizza and just indulged in the brownie sundae. "I know what you mean."

A gentle September breeze caressed her hair and Hank stood on the front porch beside her, wagging his tail. He'd love having Sara here too, Sadie thought to herself, because it meant some extra walks for him and someone else willing to play fetch with his favorite rag toy.

Sara walked over to pet Hank, and then looked up at Sadie and Roz. "What should we do now?"

"Well," Roz said with a mischievous smile, "we could look in my mystery box and find out what's inside."

"Mystery box?" Sara echoed, her brow creased in confusion. "What's that?"

"I'll tell you all about it," Sadie said, "while we get you settled in your bedroom."

"I'll get the box out of your car," Roz said, holding out one hand. "Keys?"

Sadie dug into her pants pocket and retrieved the keys to her Tahoe. Then she tossed them to Roz.

Roz snatched them out of the air.

"Wow," Sara exclaimed. "Good catch!"

"I was the star softball player on my team for three years running," Roz told her. "They called me Quick Paws Roz."

Sara laughed as she turned to Sadie. "Is that true, Grandma?"

"It sure is," Sadie said, laughing with her. She grabbed Sara's suitcase and steered her toward the stairs. "We'll be right back down, Roz."

"Take your time," Roz said, heading toward the front door with Hank by her side. "That will build the anticipation."

As they mounted the stairs, Sara said, "So what do you think is in the mystery box, Grandma?"

"I have no idea," Sadie replied, "but I hope there's something Roz likes. I've seen some mystery boxes that were real duds, with stuff that should have gone into a trash can instead of a mystery box. But once in a while you can find a hidden treasure or two."

When they reached the landing at the top of the stairs, Sadie turned to Sara. "Which bedroom do you want to stay in?" She had decorated each of the three guest bedrooms with a particular theme, with the help of Julie, an interior designer and part-time employee at the Antique Mine. One bedroom depicted a mountain theme, the second bedroom had an evergreen theme, and the third bedroom had a playful cowgirl theme.

"The cowgirl room," Sara said without hesitation. "It's been a while since I've stayed in that one."

"Then the cowgirl room it is." Sadie walked with her down the hallway. Fortunately, she'd given each bedroom a quick dusting and airing early that morning in anticipation of Sara's arrival.

They entered the room and Sadie set Sara's suitcase on the blue-and-white patchwork bed quilt that was appliquéd with horseshoes and stars. Sara placed her backpack on the hitching post that served as a coatrack and then walked over to the window and lifted the drape to reveal the grassy meadow below and the sun setting behind the snowcapped mountain peaks. The painted sky was lit in lovely pastels of pinks, purples, and blues. Sadie knew that only God could create something so glorious.

"We should take Daisy and Scout out for a ride while I'm here," Sara said, referring to the horses that she and Sadie boarded at Milo Henderson's ranch.

Sadie smiled. "That's a wonderful idea. Maybe we can go next weekend and take one of the longer trails. I could pack us a picnic lunch."

"Sounds like a good plan." Sara walked to the bedroom door. "I'll unpack my suitcase later. I want to see what's inside Roz's mystery box."

"Me too."

They made their way downstairs and found Roz and Hank waiting for them in the living room. Roz had set the mystery box on top of the coffee table and taken a seat on the sofa.

Hank lay near the fireplace, his head resting on his front paws. Sadie considered starting a fire in the hearth, since the nights were growing chillier, but the mystery box came first. She sat down next to Roz.

"I think we're ready," Sara said, plopping into a chair and draping one skinny, jean-clad leg over the side.

"All right," Roz said, scooting toward the edge of the sofa and reaching for the box lid. "Here we go."

Sadie watched with anticipation as Roz removed the remaining security tape on the box and then lifted the cardboard lid and set it aside. Both she and Sara leaned forward as Roz dipped her hand inside the box and drew out the first item.

"A Sears and Roebuck fall and winter catalog," Roz announced, squinting through her cat-eye glasses at the front cover. "Dated 1956."

"Wow, that's old," Sara said. "And kind of cool."

"Very cool." Sadie smiled. "Those catalogs are popular collectibles with a lot of my customers. It's almost worth the price of the mystery box already."

"*Ka-ching!*" Roz exclaimed, setting the catalog on the table before reaching into the box again.

This time she pulled out a black ink sketch of a bird on white paper. It was about five-by-seven inches in size and framed with black matting. The drawing was encased in a plastic bag.

"Oh my," Roz breathed, staring at the sketch. "This is nice. I'm not a big fan of bird pictures, but this one looks very well done."

Sara hopped off the chair and knelt next to Roz, her gaze on the drawing. "It's a mountain chickadee. Dr. Armstead has a big picture of one hanging on his office wall."

Roz glanced at the girl. "Do you like it?"

"I love it!" Sara said.

Roz smiled at her. "Then you can have it."

Sara's mouth opened as she looked at Roz. "Really?"

"Of course." Roz handed her the drawing. "You'll appreciate it much more than I will. And Roscoe told me that if I hang one more thing on the walls of our house, he's going to move into his hardware store."

Sadie laughed. "That's funny, considering his store has tools on the wall from floor to ceiling."

"That's what I told him," Roz said with a grin. Then she turned back to the box. "Looks like there's some newspapers, pamphlets, and other junk. They probably put them in here as filler."

"Are they old papers and pamphlets?" Sadie asked.

"Nope." Roz held them up for Sadie and Sara to see. "Looks like they're from a few months ago and the pamphlets are from some of the local attractions around Breckenridge." She put the newspapers on the floor beside her and then began paging through the pamphlets. "We've got the Country Boy Mine, Drover Dell Diner, Carter Park and Pavilion, TenMile Flyer Zipline, Mountain Top Children's Museum, the National Repertory Orchestra, and a bunch of others."

"Well, that's disappointing," Sadie said. "Is there anything else in there?"

After pulling out another handful of newspapers, Roz leaned over to look in the box and then her eyes widened. "Score!"

"What is it?" Sara asked excitedly.

"A hippie necklace!" Roz pulled out a long strand of turquoise beads strung on hemp with a silver peace symbol medallion in the center. She hung it around her neck and then stood up and posed like a fashion model. "Well, how does it look?"

"Cool," Sara chimed.

Roz bent down to pluck a small sherbet-orange bracelet out of the box. "Well, this certainly isn't vintage. In fact, it looks like it's a toy bracelet of some type."

Sadie could see the item was made of plastic and almost resembled a watch, although there was no dial on the top of the bracelet, just a circle of dark orange.

"Uh, guys…that's not a bracelet or a toy," Sara chimed in. "It's a tracking device."

Both women turned to look at her.

"How do you know that?" Sadie asked her.

"One of the kids I babysit wears one. She's five and it has a GPS chip in it. Her mom makes her wear it whenever she goes outside to play. That way, if she wanders off and gets lost, her mom can track her down."

"Is it on now?" Sadie asked her, looking at the orange bracelet.

"Probably," Sara replied. "As far as I know, there's no way to turn it off."

Roz smiled. "Well, that's certainly a strange item to find in a mystery box, although I am tempted to have Roscoe wear it around town so I can keep track of him."

"Orange isn't his color," Sadie teased, certain that Roscoe wouldn't be caught dead wearing such a thing. Despite her joke, Sadie was a little unsettled at the thought of a tracking device in her house. Had someone just thrown it inside the box, unaware of its use?

Then she remembered the blue sedan they'd thought was following them from Breckenridge. And the loose security tape on the mystery box. A slight shiver coursed through her at the thought of someone using that orange GPS bracelet to track their whereabouts.

"What's wrong?" Roz asked, studying her.

"Nothing," Sadie said, trying to hide her unease with a smile. The photo she'd taken with Roz's phone hadn't turned out well enough to determine the license plate number, so there was no way to know for sure who had been following them. She decided to change the subject. "So are you happy with your mystery box purchase?"

The answer was apparent in Roz's wide grin. "I'm thrilled. It almost makes me wish I'd bid on the other three mystery boxes, because I'm wondering what I missed out on!"

"Me too," Sara exclaimed, and then she turned to Sadie. "Why didn't you buy a mystery box, Grandma?"

"Because I've been burned by them one too many times," Sadie said wryly. "The last one I bought was just full of junk like those newspapers and pamphlets."

Roz nodded. "I got lucky this time, Sara. Although your grandma did find a treasure at the auction." She turned to Sadie. "Have you shown her yet?"

"Not yet," Sadie said. "I was afraid if I got the teddy bear out, I'd be up until the wee hours of the morning with it."

Sara held both hands up in the air. "Whoa, wait a minute. Grandma, you bought a stuffed animal?"

Sadie smiled at the confusion on her granddaughter's face. "Not just any stuffed animal. It's a Steiff teddy bear. They're collectible, and this one seems to be in excellent condition."

Sara's hazel eyes widened in appreciation. "You mean, it's like the Steiff teddy bear I used to play with?"

"Yep, just a different color," Sadie told her. "Shall we take a peek at it?"

"Only if you promise not to let it keep you up all night," Roz teased.

"I promise." Sadie rose from the sofa and walked over to the small table where she'd placed the auction bag. She pulled out the teddy bear and removed the protective plastic before carrying the bear back to the living room.

This was the first time she'd seen the teddy bear outside of the plastic barrier, giving her a good chance to look more closely at the construction. She was amazed at the impeccable condition of the teddy bear. The fur wasn't discolored or patchy, and its black boot-button eyes, which appeared to be original, gleamed in the lamplight. Whoever had owned this teddy bear had obviously cherished it and given it very good care.

"Here it is." She handed the teddy bear to Sara. As she did so, Sadie noticed a piece of brown thread, about three inches long, hanging from the bottom seam of the bear's torso. Sadie leaned closer. "Hold on," she said, taking it back from her granddaughter.

"What's wrong?" Sara asked her.

"There's a loose thread." Sadie carefully followed the thread to the seam, taking care not to pull on it. Then she parted the fur on the seam and noticed that a small sewing repair had been made there. The new thread appeared to be a shade darker than the original thread on the rest of the teddy bear's seams. That told her a restoration specialist for antiques and collectibles had not done the repair.

"How bad is it?" Roz asked.

"It doesn't appear bad at all, thankfully." Sadie handed the teddy bear back to Sara. "There are seven or eight loose stitches, but nothing I can't fix."

"It's so cute," Sara observed, carefully turning the teddy bear around in her hands. "And this Steiff person invented the teddy bear, right?"

Sadie smiled, always ready to give a history lesson. "Steiff is the name of a nineteenth-century toy company founded by Margarete Steiff," she explained. "Margarete actually got started designing pincushions shaped like elephants and was surprised when they became popular as toys for children. Without the pins, of course."

"I should hope so," Roz said, chuckling.

"But it was Margarete's nephew, Richard, who designed the teddy bear in 1902," Sadie continued. "The popularity of the stuffed bears skyrocketed, and that's what made the company famous."

"Wow, Grandma, you know a lot about teddy bears," Sara said.

"I guess I know more than the average bear," Sadie said, with a wink toward Roz. Then she turned back to Sara. "When your grandpa took me to Germany for our twenty-fifth wedding anniversary, we toured the original Steiff factory in Giengen and learned so much about their production. So these teddy bears have always held a special place in my heart."

"Cool," Sara said.

Roz began packing up her mystery box. "Have you decided if you're going to keep the teddy bear, Sadie, or put it up for sale in your shop?"

"I'm going to sell the bear. I already have one of my own, so I can't justify keeping it." Sadie picked up the newspapers from the floor. Then she turned to Roz and held them out to her. "Do you want these?"

"No, you can throw them away." Roz placed the stack of pamphlets on the sofa between them. "These too. Along with the GPS tracking device." She added the orange bracelet to the top of the pamphlets. "I don't have any use for them."

"I might put the pamphlets in my shop." Sadie picked up the pamphlets and tapped them together on the arm of the sofa. "They're in good condition and some of the tourists might find them useful."

Sara opened her mouth in a wide yawn, showing off her braces, which she usually tried to hide. "I'm so tired and I still have a chapter in my history book to read tonight."

Sadie smiled. "Well then, you'd better get to it."

"I think I'll read it in bed," Sara said. "History always puts me to sleep."

Sadie placed a hand over her heart and feigned despair. "As a former history teacher, you don't know how much those words wound me, child."

Sara grinned. "Sorry, Grandma, but I can't lie." Then she rose to her feet and set the teddy bear on the coffee table before turning to Roz. "Thanks again for the drawing, Roz. I love it."

Roz reached over to give Sara's arm an affectionate squeeze. "You're welcome, dear."

"Good night," Sara said, heading toward the stairs.

"Good night," Sadie and Roz called after her.

Hank lifted his head at the sound of Sara's footsteps on the stairs. He stood up and padded after her, his tail wagging behind him.

"I should probably get going too," Roz said, lifting the box in her arms. "I might even hide this box before Roscoe gets home from bowling. He doesn't understand why I like spending money on 'junk' as he calls it."

Sadie chuckled as she walked Roz to the front door, knowing her friend would show off the items in her mystery box to Roscoe before breakfast the next morning.

They stepped out onto the front porch. Stars were just starting to appear in the night sky, and a cool breeze caressed Sadie's face, bringing with it the scent of fresh pine. "Thanks again for coming to the auction with me today."

"It was my pleasure." Roz walked to her car and placed the box in the backseat. Then she turned and gave Sadie a wave. "See you soon!"

"'Bye."

Sadie stayed on the porch and watched Roz drive off, enjoying the serenity of the night. The rustle of leaves in the aspen trees whispered around her as Sadie stared up at the sky. A stanza from one of her favorite hymns came to her lips, inspired by the glory of nature surrounding her.

"For the beauty of each hour,
of the day and of the night,
hill and vale, and tree and flower,
sun and moon and stars of light;
Lord of all, to Thee we raise
this our hymn of grateful praise."

The gentle breeze carried away her words as she sang the first stanza softly under her breath. After one last look at the bright stars sparkling in the night sky, Sadie turned around and walked back inside the house.

Her gaze fell on the table where Roz had left the stack of newspapers. On top of them sat the orange GPS bracelet.

Sadie stared at it for a long moment, wondering if someone was receiving a signal from the GPS device that would lead them right to her house.

Now she just had to decide what to do about it.

4

———

THE NEXT MORNING, SADIE WOKE UP EARLIER THAN USUAL, STILL a little disturbed by the GPS tracking device that they'd found in Roz's mystery box.

After brushing her teeth, Sadie got dressed and made her way down the second-floor hallway, stopping a moment to take a peek through the half-open door of the cowgirl room. Sara lay buried under the blankets in bed, her back to the door and her arms wrapped around the spare pillow, still sound asleep.

"At least one of us can sleep," Sadie murmured quietly as she turned from the doorway and made her way downstairs. Hank met her at the bottom of the stairs and then led the way into the kitchen. Sadie knew a cup of hot tea and her daily devotional would ease the tension inside of her.

A few minutes later, she sat down at the kitchen table, her teacup in hand and her devotional book and Bible in front of her. She set the cup down and opened the devotional with a sigh of contentment. Then she read the verse for the day from Psalm 28:7: "The Lord is my strength and my shield; my heart trusted in him, and I am helped: therefore my heart greatly rejoiceth; and with my song will I praise him."

The words soothed her and reminded her that trusting the Lord was always the answer. She leaned back in her chair and took a sip of the hot tea as she continued with the devotional, ending it with a heartfelt prayer. Then she turned to Hank, who sat patiently beside her chair.

"I hope you're ready for a long walk today." She reached out her hands to scratch behind both of his furry ears. "We're going all the way up to the creek."

Hank bounded to the back door leading out of the kitchen and then turned to watch her, his tail wagging furiously behind him.

Sadie laughed before draining her teacup and rising from the table. She carried her cup over to the sink and rinsed it out. Then she grabbed her North Face jacket off the hook by the door and walked outside with Hank sprinting ahead of her.

Before locking the door behind her, Sadie decided to step back inside the house and retrieve the orange GPS bracelet that she'd left on the pile of newspapers.

The bracelet remained where she'd left it last night, looking much more like a toy than a tracking device. She slipped it on her wrist and looked at it for a long moment. Then she walked to the back door and locked it behind her before hurrying to catch up with Hank. He hadn't gone far, just to the edge of the back gate. They walked together over the mountain road and onto the trail.

Sadie inhaled the cold morning air and quickly zipped up her jacket. Then she dug into the pockets for her leather gloves, pulling them on to her cold hands.

Hank bounded around the thick, leafy bushes along the trail. Some leaves and brush carpeted the trail, making a familiar crunch beneath her hiking shoes. A heavy mist hung over the mountains and Sadie could just glimpse the yellow glow of the rising sun through the misty layer of clouds in the east.

A rabbit, spooked by Hank's frolicking in the heavy brush, hopped out in front of Sadie, its white tail bouncing rapidly over the trail before it disappeared into the brush again. Hank gave chase for a while, but the rabbit was too small and quick for him to keep up.

The dog circled back on the trail as Sadie started walking up the steep incline that led to the creek. Her breath came out in white puffs of frosty air as she walked, but her feet were warm in the thick, woolen socks and hiking shoes she'd donned this morning.

The mile-and-a-half trek to the creek was mostly uphill and afforded Sadie some of the most beautiful views around Silver Peak. She'd seen deer on the trail in the past, and even some longhorn sheep. A majestic, red-shouldered hawk flew overhead, circling a tall grove of fir trees in the distance before flying out of sight.

Despite the cold weather, the climb up the trail warmed Sadie quickly. She kept her gloves on, but unzipped her jacket halfway and inhaled a deep breath of fresh air.

Then her gaze fell on a small, bare tree branch on the trail. It was about one inch in circumference and a foot and a half long. "Hey, Hank," she called out, bending down to pick up the stick. "Look what I found."

Hank emerged from the brush a few yards ahead of her. Then he scampered toward her, his big brown eyes on the stick in her hand. He began to jump around her, emitting soft, excited barks.

"Ready to play some fetch?" she asked, holding the stick up in the air and then giving it a strong toss. It landed somewhere in the bushes a few yards away and Hank quickly followed in pursuit.

Sadie found herself smiling as she continued up the trail, certain that Hank wouldn't be far behind.

Less than a minute later, Hank was back by her side with the stick tucked in his mouth.

"Good boy," she said, leaning down to pet him and picking a few stray leaves off his fur.

Hank dropped the stick at her feet and then looked up at Sadie, his tail wagging behind him.

She smiled. "Something tells me we're going to play this game all the way to the creek." Sadie picked up the stick and tossed it even farther this time. Then Hank ran in the same direction.

A small flock of robins fluttered in the bushes and soon took flight, rousted by Hank's sudden dash through the brush. Sadie continued up the trail, becoming more aware of the orange GPS bracelet on her wrist.

Hank returned again and again, dropping the stick at Sadie's feet and waiting until she threw it again to chase after it.

"He doesn't need a GPS tracker to find it," she said out loud as she continued on her way to the creek.

The sun peeked through the clouds, burning some of the mist away. The forecast promised an afternoon high in the mid-fifties, with sunny skies and a light breeze. The only shadow on the day ahead was deciding what to do with the GPS bracelet. There could be a lot of reasons it had been in that mystery box, Sadie thought to herself. Reasons that were innocent and not-so-innocent.

Sadie began to list the possible reasons out loud, mindlessly tossing the stick each time Hank brought it back to her.

"Maybe it was put in there inadvertently," she ventured. "Someone thought it was just a bracelet, or didn't know what it was and decided just to throw it in the box. Or maybe they'd used it as a GPS tracker but didn't need it anymore."

Sadie unzipped her jacket all the way, the bright sun warming her now as she walked. "GPS devices are used in geocaching," she reminded herself.

She'd learned about geocaching from Alice, who had been active in the contemporary sport for several years while she was married to Cliff. It was like a modern-day treasure hunt, where participants were given coordinates and then used a GPS device to lead them to the "treasure." According to Alice, that treasure could be anything from lollipops to fancy jewelry and everything in between.

"Maybe someone in the Ferris family was active in that sport and used the bracelet as their GPS device."

But as Sadie looked at the orange bracelet, she couldn't figure out how it would be used for geocaching, since it didn't have a screen or any place to type in coordinates. No, this bracelet-like GPS device on her wrist was meant to keep track of the person wearing it.

Hank now trotted along beside her on the trail, the stick clamped in his mouth, until Sadie stopped and wedged it free before tossing it again. She could hear the gurgle of the creek now and knew they were close. The sun had cleared away most of the mist and the blue sky above seemed to go on forever.

She sighed, slipping the orange bracelet off her wrist and tucking it into the pocket of her jacket. She'd been worried ever since Roz had pulled it out of the mystery box last night and Sara had revealed its purpose. Perhaps Sadie wouldn't have cared if she hadn't remembered the blue sedan creeping behind them yesterday and the loose security tape on the mystery box when they'd picked it up.

"But, really," she said out loud. "Why would anyone want to follow us?" The idea seemed ludicrous on its face. She couldn't think of one person at the Ferris estate auction who would have any reason to follow her or Roz.

But someone who wasn't at the auction might have a reason. That thought made her stop in her tracks. Sadie stood there for a long moment, until Hank's cold nose dug into her palm. She looked down to see the stick lying at her feet. Sadie bent over to pick it up and toss it as far up the trail as she could throw it. Hank took off after it, leaving Sadie behind.

She started walking again, considering the possibility that Leo Best, Marv's business partner—or rather, former business partner—might have been responsible for the GPS tracker in the mystery box.

According to what Herbert had told her, Leo was suing Marvin. Perhaps he—or a private investigator in his employ—had wanted to track some of Marvin's customers to verify that the financials were on the up-and-up. But that would mean planting more than one GPS tracker among the items sold at the auction.

Perhaps Marvin had even been contacted by one of the other winners at the auction about another GPS tracker. She made a mental note to contact him and find a way to ask that question without sounding crazy.

By the time Sadie reached the creek, she realized that she couldn't relax as long as the orange GPS bracelet was around. There was no reason for her to keep it—especially when she didn't know whether someone had placed it in that box to track her or Roz.

Hank appeared on the trail with the stick in his mouth and trotted up to Sadie. He dropped it at her feet and then sat down.

"Good boy," she said, reaching out to pat his head. "Let's both take a rest before we head back, okay?"

Hank replied with a loud yawn. Then he padded over to the creek and began lapping up the crystal-clear water.

Sadie took the GPS bracelet from her pocket, ready to get rid of it. If someone had planted it in the mystery box, then they could have fun searching these mountains for the signal. She reared her arm back and flung the bracelet as far as she could throw it.

Like a flash, Hank ran off in that direction.

"Hank," Sadie called after him, realizing too late that he'd think this was just another game of fetch. She watched him splash his way across the shallow creek until he made it to the other side, then he disappeared into a thicket of trees.

Sadie shook her head, a smile curving her mouth. Moments later, Hank reappeared, splashing his way across the creek once more before proudly dropping the orange bracelet at her feet.

"You silly dog," she said, rubbing the length of his back. The rest of him was soaking wet, but his heavy coat made him impervious to any chill. Hank looked up at her, his tail wagging, waiting to play another game of fetch.

"Sorry, buddy," she said, bending down to pick up the bracelet. "It's time to go home. And we're not taking this thing with us."

She commanded him to sit. When Hank obeyed, she looked at him sternly and said, "Stay." Then she hurled the GPS bracelet once more into the thicket of trees.

Hank whined and moved restlessly against the hand she'd placed on his head. But he didn't chase after the bracelet.

After a few moments, Sadie started back down the trail toward the house and Hank followed along beside her.

The trip downhill moved a little faster, but Sadie had to be careful not to slip on any damp leaves on the trail. Hank dove in and out of the brush alongside the trail, sometimes falling behind and other times dashing far ahead before running back to Sadie's side.

As she walked, Sadie thought about what she should make Sara for breakfast. It wasn't often that she had an overnight guest, and she looked forward to spoiling her granddaughter just a little. As she considered different recipes, Sadie tried to remember exactly what ingredients she had available in her pantry and refrigerator.

She'd been walking back down the trail for about five minutes when she suddenly realized that Hank wasn't beside her. She stopped for a moment and looked around, expecting him to pop out from the brush on either side of the trail, but the longer she waited, the more concerned she became. At last, she began to call for him. "Hank! Hank, where are you? Come here, boy!"

She waited a minute or two, but there was still no sign of him. Sadie couldn't even hear him rumbling through the brush. "Hank!"

She was more puzzled by his disappearance than worried about it. Hank knew these mountains—and especially this trail— better than Sadie did. He could also take care of himself—as more than one tussle with the local wildlife had proven. But it wasn't like him to simply vanish like this.

"Hank!" she called out again.

Then she heard the sound of crunching leaves behind her and she turned to see Hank trotting down the trail toward her. He had the orange GPS bracelet in his mouth.

Sadie was both relieved and amused. "When you play fetch, you're determined to win, aren't you?"

Sadie took the orange bracelet from him and slipped it into her pocket, considering the possibility that this meant she wasn't supposed to get rid of it just yet.

"Thanks, boy," she said, ruffling the damp fur on his neck. "Now let's go home."

5

LATER THAT MORNING, SADIE UNLOCKED THE FRONT DOOR OF the Antique Mine and walked inside. She loved her shop, and the sight of all her lovely antiques and collectibles always gave her an extra bounce in her step. She inhaled the aroma of polished wood and let her gaze fall on the colorful vintage fabrics and linens that brightened the shelves.

She hummed to herself as she carried the Steiff teddy bear and the stack of pamphlets over to the front counter. After setting them down, she slipped her purse off her shoulder and placed it behind the desk, along with her jacket. Then she finger-combed her short salt-and-pepper hair, which had been ruffled by a sudden, brisk wind sweeping through town.

Her morning walk with Hank had lasted almost two hours and they'd made it all the way to the creek by the old family silver mine. Now that she'd had time to think about it, she was glad that Hank had fetched the orange GPS bracelet and brought it back to her. If someone had planted that GPS device in the mystery box, they would have had had plenty of time to track the device to her house, so there was really no more danger in keeping it. More likely, it was tossed in the box by someone who had no idea of its purpose and was perfectly innocuous.

By the time Sadie and Hank had returned from the walk, Sara had been up and showered and was texting on her phone in the kitchen. Sadie had enjoyed chatting with her granddaughter while washing a few dishes and had even talked Sara into borrowing one of her fleece jackets to wear to school, since the girl had left home without one.

While Sara had finished getting ready for school, Sadie had dug through her spare closets until she'd found a simple white fleece jacket that wouldn't embarrass the fourteen-year-old too much. Then she'd sent Sara off to school after feeding her a hearty breakfast of blueberry pancakes, bacon, and scrambled eggs.

Sadie made a quick trip into Arbuckle's next door to buy a large cup of coffee and then returned to the Antique Mine and started to plan her day. The first thing on her agenda was making a thorough examination of the Steiff teddy bear.

After her hike earlier this morning, she'd spent some time on the computer researching Steiff teddy bears made in 1907. The information she'd discovered about them made it clear that she'd gotten a real bargain at the auction. This morning, she planned to repair the loose torso seam stitches and then put the teddy bear up for sale in her shop.

Sadie took a sip of the delicious coffee and then headed to the front counter to switch on the computer.

As the computer was booting up, she left her coffee on the counter and carried the teddy bear into the back room. She pulled the teddy bear from its plastic bag and set it in one of the clean, plastic trays that she often used for the restoration process.

With a pair of small, sewing scissors, Sadie carefully snipped the loose brown thread hanging from the inner leg seam. Then she went in search of a matching spool of brown thread by looking in each drawer of the front counter.

The bell above the front door tinkled, and Sadie walked out of the back room to see her pastor's wife, Jeanne Sweeting, walking into the shop.

"Good morning," Sadie greeted her. "A little blustery out there today, isn't it?"

"That wind just about blew me away," Jeanne said, a fashionable yellow knit shawl draped around her shoulders. "And it's cold enough to remind us that winter is lurking right around the corner."

"It's supposed to warm up this afternoon, but I do like the changing seasons." Sadie picked up her coffee cup. "By the time a new season does come around, I'm always ready for it."

"Me too," Jeanne said, walking to the front counter. "And speaking of seasons, I'm looking for a birthday gift for Don's secretary, Mary Sue, who loves all things Christmas. So I was hoping you might have some vintage Christmas ornaments or something else with a Christmas theme that she might like."

"As a matter of fact, I do," Sadie said with a smile. She knew Mary Sue was a hard worker and someone who didn't spend much money on frills. "I haven't set any Christmas items out on display yet, but there are some in the back. Just give me a minute, and I'll bring them out."

"Take as long as you like," Jeanne said, running one slender hand over her smooth, mocha forehead. "You know how much I love to look around your shop."

Sadie left Jeanne to browse and walked into the back room. It took a moment for her to locate the Christmas ornaments, but she found a box of them on a top shelf and used a step stool to reach it and take it down. Then she spent the next several minutes carefully unwrapping the protective Bubble Wrap from each of the delicate glass ornaments. She layered a piece of white cotton batting on a plastic tray to provide a nice cushion before placing the ornaments in the tray. Then she carried the tray out to the front counter.

"Here we are," Sadie called out to Jeanne, who was fingering a handmade lace pillowcase. "I have about a dozen Christmas ornaments ready to choose from."

"That sounds perfect." Jeanne walked over to the front counter and gasped in delight when she saw the ornaments in the tray. "Oh, Sadie, they're lovely! I'm sure Mary Sue would be thrilled with any of these."

Sadie smiled. "Now comes the hard part—choosing which one you want."

Jeanne sighed. "You're right about that. I'm drawn to this one," she said, pointing to a midnight-blue glass ball with sparkling silver beads and a silver tassel hanging from the bottom. "But I know green is Mary Sue's favorite color, so she might prefer this ornament." Jeanne carefully picked up an emerald green ornament with gold and red accents and a gold, silk tassel.

"They're both beautiful," Sadie observed. "I don't think you could go wrong with either one."

"So maybe I should buy both?" Jeanne ventured with a mischievous smile. "I'm almost afraid to ask how much they are."

"Fifteen dollars each," Sadie said, hoping that price fit into Jeanne's gift budget.

"So thirty dollars total?" Jeanne grinned. "That's just what I'd planned to spend."

"Does that mean you'd like me to wrap both of them to go?"

"It sure does." Jeanne rubbed her hands together with glee.

"Excellent." Sadie reached for the small roll of Bubble Wrap that she kept behind the front counter. "And I happen to have a vintage Christmas box that's just the right size for these ornaments. I'll throw in it for free if you'd like."

Jeanne placed one hand over her heart. "Thank you, Sadie. This is going to be the perfect gift for Mary Sue."

As Sadie rung up the sale, she thought about how difficult it often was to find the perfect gift for another adult, especially as she and her friends got older. Sadie didn't want for much, and usually she just purchased the things she did want.

Roz and Alice had each recently asked her what she'd like for her birthday, which was only a couple of weeks away, but Sadie honestly couldn't think of a single thing. At her age, the pleasure of good company far outweighed most material things.

Another customer entered the shop, setting off the bell. Sadie glanced up to see a young woman she didn't recognize, although the girl had striking features. She looked about twenty years old, and her big, dark eyes filled a flawless face with chiseled cheekbones and a tiny beauty mark near one corner of her mouth. As the woman approached the front counter, Sadie estimated her height to be slightly above six feet—close to that of her friend Roz. Her long legs were clad in black, skintight jeans, and she wore a tunic-style, white chiffon blouse.

"Good morning," Sadie greeted her new customer. "I'll be with you in just a moment."

"No need," the young woman said as she wandered toward an old butter churn. "I'll have fun just looking around. You have some amazing things here."

"Thank you," Sadie said before turning her attention back to Jeanne. "Is there anything else you'd like today?"

Jeanne smiled. "No, I think this will do just fine."

Sadie retrieved the vintage Christmas box from the back room and brought it to the front counter. Then she carefully packed the wrapped ornaments inside before adding the lid and handing the box to Jeanne. "You'll have to let me know how Mary Sue likes her gift."

"I will," Jeanne promised as she turned and headed toward the door. "Thanks again, Sadie!"

"You're welcome," Sadie called after her. "See you Sunday!"

A brisk gust of wind blew through the shop when Jeanne opened the door. Sadie watched her hold tight to the brass doorknob as she pulled the door closed.

The young woman in her shop was now busy looking at pewter candlestick holders on a shelf near the chimney stove, so Sadie walked to the back room to search for her reparation supplies. It didn't take her long to find a spool of brown thread that matched the original thread on the teddy bear.

Sadie picked up her portable sewing kit and the tray with the teddy bear before walking back to the front counter in case the woman needed assistance. Since her customer was still browsing, she unspooled a few inches of thread, holding it tight against the leg seam of the teddy bear to test the color. The thread appeared invisible, which meant it was an almost perfect match.

Sadie pulled a needle from her sewing kit and expertly threaded it with the brown thread, tying a knot at the end. Before she began sewing the seam with the new thread, she needed to remove the light brown thread that had been used for the initial repair.

"Excuse me?"

Sadie looked up to see the young woman on the other side of the front counter. She held up a pair of small pewter candlesticks. "How much are these?"

"Forty dollars," Sadie said with a smile. "I think the sticker price is on the bottom."

"Oh," the woman said, and then giggled after she turned the candlestick holders over. "Yep, it's right here. Guess I should have looked before bothering you."

"Believe me, it's no bother," Sadie assured her. "I'm always happy to answer any questions." She leaned on the counter. "And that pewter was made from silver unearthed at the local silver mines right here in Silver Peak. It's very high quality."

"They do seem quite nice." She held out her hand. "I'm Giselle, by the way. Giselle Fleur."

"It's nice to meet you, Giselle." Sadie reached over to shake her thin hand.

Sadie set the teddy bear on the counter between them. "Do you live in Silver Peak?"

"Oh no," Giselle replied. "I could never live any place this small. I'm originally from Denver, but I'm on my way to New York City to become a fashion model."

There was a naïveté about the girl that made Sadie want to take her under her wing and warn her away from the cutthroat world of fashion modeling. But Giselle was an adult and probably wouldn't appreciate advice from a stranger. "That sounds exciting."

"I just turned twenty, so it's now or never," Giselle said, setting the pewter candlestick holders on the counter.

"So what brings you to Silver Peak today?"

Giselle hesitated. "I'm scoping out some different places to shoot for my portfolio. I need a few more photos before I can send it to modeling agencies in New York. And photographers are much cheaper here than there."

"Well, we're glad to have you here. There are some lovely locations that would be perfect for a photo shoot."

Giselle flipped her long, dark hair over one shoulder. "Yes, I've already gotten some ideas. I decided to stop in here to find a souvenir to take with me to New York. I want something to help me remember where I came from once I make it big."

Sadie swallowed a sigh. She believed people should pursue their dreams—that's why she'd opened the Antique Mine after so many years as a high school history and business teacher. And Giselle truly *was* beautiful and statuesque enough to be a model. She just hoped Giselle's dreams wouldn't lead to heartache and disappointment.

Giselle's big brown eyes widened as she looked over the marble countertop. "Oh, wow! That teddy bear is super cute!"

"He is adorable, isn't he?" Sadie picked up the teddy bear and held it up so the young woman could have a better look at it. "I just bought him at an estate sale in Breckenridge yesterday. It's a Steiff teddy bear made in 1907."

Giselle's mouth gaped. "That was over a century ago."

"Before I was born, that's for sure," Sadie said with a smile. She set the teddy bear carefully on the counter and then turned toward the pewter candlestick holders.

"So did you want to purchase these candlestick holders?" Sadie asked, reaching for them.

"No, thank you," Giselle said with a smile. "Actually, I want the teddy bear."

Sadie's hand froze in midair. Then she pulled it back. "The teddy bear?" She wasn't quite ready to sell it, so she tried to deter Giselle. "I'm afraid it's pretty expensive."

"How much?"

Sadie mentally calculated the retail price, although she doubted a twenty-year-old, aspiring model could afford an original Steiff. "Twenty-four hundred dollars."

"Okay," Giselle said without missing a beat. She reached into her purse and pulled out a billfold. "You take cash, right?"

Sadie blinked. "Yes, I do."

"Perfect." Giselle counted out twenty-four crisp, hundred-dollar bills and handed them to Sadie.

"There are a few loose threads that I need to fix on the teddy bear," Sadie said, still shocked by the quick sale. "I should be done in about an hour if you want to stop back in and pick it up."

"Oh, that's all right," Giselle said with a carefree shrug. "I'll just take it with me now and get it fixed somewhere else."

"Are you sure?" Sadie asked. "You'll have to pay for a repair somewhere else while I'm happy to fix it for free."

"I'm positive." Giselle plucked a cell phone from her pocket and looked at the screen. "I'm on my way out of town and really need to get going."

"You could pick the teddy bear up when you come back for your photo shoot," Sadie suggested, not wanting to send the Steiff away in disrepair.

"No, that's okay," Giselle told her. "I'm not positive I'm even coming back here. I put up some photographs of myself on a

Web site that agents look at to find models. I could get the call any day from New York or Paris."

Sadie sensed that Giselle was determined to take the teddy bear with her, no matter what services Sadie offered. After adding the money to the cash register, she carefully placed the teddy bear back in the plastic sack. "I'm going to put this thread in the sack too," she told Giselle, holding up the spool of brown thread. "It's the perfect match to the original thread, so whoever finishes the seam repair will be ready to go."

"Okay," Giselle said with another shrug.

Sadie placed both items in a larger, paper bag with a handle and then handed it over to Giselle. "I hope you enjoy the teddy bear."

"Oh, I will," Giselle said. "Thanks again."

Sadie watched her leave, feeling a little let down that she couldn't spend more time with the teddy bear. She'd been looking forward to seeing it on display in the Antique Mine, secretly hoping it wouldn't sell for a while. She sighed, resigning herself to the fact that it was gone and wondering if she'd ever see Giselle's lovely face in a magazine.

When the shop was empty, Sadie looked around, wondering what to do next. She spied the pamphlets from the mystery box on the counter and put them away in one of the desk drawers. She'd sort through them later and decide where to put them. At the moment, she wanted to dig into her back room and take stock of her autumn-themed collectibles.

Then she looked up and saw Edwin walking into her shop from Arbuckle's. He held a coffee cup in one hand and had a twinkle in his blue eyes. "Good morning, Sadie. I had a few minutes between meetings, so I thought I'd stop for coffee and a chat with the prettiest Antique Lady in town."

Sadie blushed. "Well, I'm sure glad you did."

"So tell me about the auction yesterday. Did you get that phonograph you wanted so much?"

She shook her head. "No. Sadly, I was outbid. I was going to call you last night, but Sara came to stay with me a day early, so I didn't get a chance."

"Well, at least your day had a silver lining."

"Two silver linings, actually." She smiled. "They had a Steiff teddy bear at the auction that hadn't made it into the sale catalog."

He arched a silver brow. "And you got it?"

"I did, and it was in excellent condition. I'd love to show it to you, but it's already gone."

"Gone?" He set down his cup. "What happened?"

"I sold it this morning." Then she told him about Giselle and how much the young woman had wanted the Steiff teddy bear.

"Sounds like you made a tidy profit," he said with a smile.

"I did," Sadie agreed, "but I wish I could have enjoyed the teddy bear for at least a few days before selling it."

"And I wish I had time to take you to lunch today to help you feel better." He took a long sip of his coffee. "Are you free tomorrow?"

"Julie is scheduled to work, so I should be."

"Wonderful. Then it's a date." He headed out of the shop, turning at the open doorway and giving her a playful wink. "I'll see you soon, Sadie."

"Sounds good," she said with a smile.

That evening, Sadie walked into the house, ready to spend the evening with her granddaughter. She'd given Sara a spare house key and saw her backpack sitting on the floor next to the front door.

Hank trotted up to greet Sadie, his pink tongue hanging out of one side of his mouth.

"Hey, buddy," she said, leaning down to pet him. "Where's that girl of ours?"

Hank wagged his tail and moved closer to Sadie, digging his nose into her palm.

"We'll go for a walk later," she promised him. "First, I need to make supper."

Sadie shed her coat and purse, then she and Hank made their way into the kitchen. Remnants of a snack of oatmeal raisin cookies and chocolate milk sat on the kitchen table, but Sara wasn't in the kitchen either.

Sadie began making the enchilada casserole she'd planned for dinner. Fifteen minutes later, she slid the casserole dish into the oven and set the temperature and the timer. Then she washed her hands at the kitchen sink, peering out the back window in search of her granddaughter. When she didn't see Sara there, Sadie headed out of the kitchen and up the stairs to the second floor.

The door to the cowgirl room was closed, so Sadie lightly tapped on the wood. "Sara?"

There was no answer.

Perplexed, Sadie turned the doorknob and pushed the door open, wondering if her granddaughter was taking a nap. Sadie had done the same thing herself a time or two after coming home from work, but when she poked her head into her room, the bed was empty.

Sara was nowhere in sight.

6

"WHERE IS THAT GIRL?" SADIE SAID TO HERSELF AS SHE CHECKED the rest of the bedrooms on the second floor, including her own.

They were all empty too.

Sadie walked back downstairs, almost certain now that Sara must have gone outside for a walk. Or perhaps one of her friends' parents had picked her up.

But wouldn't she have asked Sadie for permission first? Or at least have left a note? Or even sent a text message? Sadie knew that was the procedure at Alice's house. As a single parent, Theo and Sara didn't always have Alice around to supervise them, but Alice insisted that they leave a note or send her a text message so she'd know where to find them.

Sadie dug her cell phone out of her purse and dialed Sara's cell phone number.

Sara's phone rang four times before the automated voice mail answered. "Hey, this is Sara. I'm busy right now, so just leave a message and I'll catch you later."

Sadie waited for the tone and then said, "Sara, this is Grandma. Where are you? Please call me as soon as you get this message."

Releasing a long sigh, Sadie slipped the cell phone into the front pocket of her khaki slacks and then turned to Hank. "Let's go take that walk now. Maybe we'll find Sara out on the trail."

Ten minutes later, Sadie and Hank crossed the road near her house and headed up one of the mountain trails. She'd changed into her hiking clothes, including an extra layer to keep off the chill of the mid-September evening. The sun shimmered on the horizon as dusk was falling. Soon it would be dark—too dark for a fourteen-year-old girl to be out on the mountain trails alone.

"Sara!" Sadie called out, still hoping her granddaughter had just gone for a walk in the woods. Sara loved nature and liked to explore the area around Sadie's house.

Sadie stood still on the trail, straining to hear a response to her call. But only the sounds of nature filled the air, not the sweet sound of Sara's voice. Maybe Sara had gone out for a walk and fallen or been injured in some way…

"Stop it," Sadie chastised herself, as worry began to gnaw at the edges of her belly. "Sara can take care of herself, even out here. She's smart as a whip and she always has her cell phone with her."

Squaring her shoulders, Sadie continued her way up the trail, determined not to overreact. She'd never been one of those grandparents who panicked if their grandchild stubbed a toe. Growing up in the Rocky Mountains wasn't for the faint of heart, and Sadie had learned early that a few scrapes, scabs, and scars were just a normal part of life.

"Sara!" Sadie shouted again, her voice echoing in the distance. And once again, there was no response.

But Sara is a city girl, Sadie reminded herself. Or was, until a few years ago when Alice had moved with the kids to Silver Peak after her divorce.

The creeping darkness of night wasn't helping Sadie's anxiety. People had been lost in the mountains before, and once darkness fell it was very difficult to find anyone.

Hank trotted ahead of her, stopping along the path every once in a while to sniff the air. That wasn't unusual, but Sadie knew that if the golden retriever caught Sara's scent, he'd take off like a shot to find her.

Dried grass and pine needles carpeted the path and crunched under her feet as she hiked up a small, grassy incline. The fresh scent of pine needles filled the air and a lone coyote howled in the distance. Usually her walks gave Sadie an inner serenity that she seldom found outside of church, but this evening was different.

She pulled her cell phone out of her pocket to check the screen. Still no call or text message from her granddaughter. Sadie had tried calling Sara twice more since the first time, but both had gone to her voice mail. She'd left two more messages, urging Sara to call her as soon as possible, along with sending a couple of text messages.

It just didn't make sense. Usually, when Sara came to Sadie's house, the girl walked around like that cell phone was glued to her hand, constantly texting her friends and classmates.

The gnawing in Sadie's belly had now turned into a solid lump of fear and worry, weighing her down and making her feel a little sick inside. Despite her best intentions, Sadie began to imagine the worst. She thought once again about the blue sedan that had followed her Tahoe on the highway for so long last night. And the GPS tracking device they'd found in Roz's mystery box.

"Let's go home," she told Hank, suddenly turning around on the trail. Her footsteps quickened, hastening their trip back to the house. Hank easily kept up with her, his tongue lolling out of his mouth as he playfully dodged around the trees, bushes, and boulders in his path.

Sadie walked across the gravel road to the front edge of her long driveway. The house was completely dark, just the way she'd left it when there was still plenty of sunlight shining through the windows. That meant Sara wasn't home yet, since she would have turned on a light.

Sadie reached for her cell phone once more. She didn't know the phone number for Sara's best friend, Mia Garza, but she knew how to get it. Sadie dialed the phone number for Los Pollitos, a Mexican restaurant owned by Mia's parents. Mia and her older sister, Elena, often worked there too.

The call was picked up on the first ring. "Good evening, Los Pollitos. This is Gloria. How may I help you?"

"Hi, Gloria," she said to Mia's mother, "this is Sadie Speers." She hesitated, not wanting to sound too panicked. "I'm trying to reach Sara and was hoping Mia could help me. Is she working there tonight by chance?"

"She is," Gloria replied. "Just hold on a moment, Sadie, while I get her."

"Thank you." Sadie nibbled her lower lip as she waited. If Mia was working at Los Pollitos, that meant Sara wasn't with her.

So where was she?

Sara had other friends, of course. Lauren or Nicole might be with Sara, so maybe Mia could give her those girls' phone numbers. Or tell her if Sara had plans for the evening that she hadn't mentioned to Sadie.

A few moments later, Mia came on the line. "Hello?"

"Hi, Mia. This is Sara's grandma. I'm sorry to bother you while you're working, but I can't find Sara and she's not answering her cell phone. Do you happen to know where she is?"

"Um, no."

Disappointment swept through Sadie. "But you saw her at school today, right?"

"Yes, we have most of our classes together."

"Did you see her leave school when your classes let out?"

"Yes, we walked out of the building together," Mia said. "Did you try sending her a text?"

"I did," Sadie replied. "Several times. And I tried calling her, too, but I just get her voice mail."

"That's weird," Mia replied. "I wish I could help you."

"That's all right," Sadie told her. Then she asked for Lauren and Nicole's cell phone numbers before ending the call.

But when Sadie phoned the other girls, neither one of them had seen Sara or talked to her since school had let out earlier that day.

"All right," she said to Hank after ending the phone call with Nicole. "Now I'm really starting to worry." She contemplated calling the police as she walked up the steps of her front porch. Maybe Sadie would give Edwin a call too, and ask him to drive around town to see if he could spot Sara.

Sadie opened the front door and Hank bolted past her, running toward the kitchen. That was when she saw the glow of light in the hallway and her heart leapt in her chest.

"Sara?" she called out, following Hank down the hall.

"I'm in the kitchen, Grandma."

The sound of her granddaughter's voice brought tears of relief and happiness to her eyes. She blinked them back before she entered the kitchen, not wanting Sara to see her reaction.

Sara sat at the table, a textbook open in front of her and her hand deep in a bowl of goldfish-shaped crackers. She looked up as Sadie walked into the kitchen.

"Don't worry," Sara said, scooping up a handful of crackers, "I won't let these ruin my dinner."

Sadie cracked a smile at that remark, aware that she'd been worried about much worse. "That's fine. But where have you been?"

Sara blinked at her. "What do you mean?"

"I couldn't find you earlier when I came home from the shop. You weren't in the house. And all the lights were out in the house just a few minutes ago."

"Oh." Sara popped a cracker into her mouth, chewing for a long moment before she finally swallowed and said, "That must have been when I was out in the backyard."

"But I looked back there."

Sara shrugged her narrow shoulders as her gaze returned to her book. "I walked around for a bit. I guess we must have just missed each other."

"I guess so," Sadie said, not quite convinced. "But what about my calls and texts? Why didn't you answer your phone?"

"Sorry. I left my phone at school," Sara said, looking sheepish. "Mr. Wolford caught me using it to look at Facebook during chemistry class and took it away. He told me I could pick up my phone from his classroom after school, but I completely forgot." She leaned forward and looked beseechingly at Sadie. "Please don't tell Mom, Grandma."

Sadie walked over to the table and placed one gentle hand on Sara's shoulder. "I won't tell her, but why don't you keep your phone in your locker at school from now on. Then you won't be tempted to look at it during class."

"I'll try," Sara said, her braces flashing as she smiled up at Sadie.

Then Sadie noticed something in Sara's strawberry-blonde hair. She reached out and picked up a thick clump of dust.

Sadie tossed the tiny dust bunny in the trash, wondering if she hadn't cleaned as well as she'd thought for Sara's arrival. But the dust didn't matter. Nothing mattered now that she knew Sara was home, safe and sound. She breathed a silent prayer of thanks and then began preparing a salad to go with the enchilada casserole.

The next morning, Sadie walked through the connecting door from her shop into Arbuckle's, ready for a tall cup of coffee. She hadn't slept well the night before and she'd even gotten up around three o'clock in the morning to check on Sara, just to reassure herself that the girl was safe in bed. Now Sadie was tired and had a slight headache, but fortunately she knew just the cure.

"Good morning, Hector," she said. "I'll take the usual. And one cinnamon bun."

Hector stood behind the counter, wearing a neatly pressed apron and a welcoming smile. "Coming right up, Sadie."

Sadie turned slightly to survey the room, waving to some friends who sat at a table in the far corner.

"Hello, Sadie," said a voice behind her.

Sadie turned to see her cousin, Laura Finch. "Well, hi there, stranger! This is a nice surprise."

Laura was about ten years younger than Sadie and had recently moved to Silver Peak from Massachusetts. They shared a love of the outdoors and often traded recipes, although Laura's East Coast style of cooking was much fancier than Sadie's rustic western fare.

"I haven't seen you since you started working on that big marketing project," Sadie said. "How have you been?"

"Just fine," Laura said, smiling. "I emerge from my cubbyhole every once in a blue moon. Arbuckle's coffee keeps me going. And so does that wonderful chili recipe you gave me." She patted her stomach. "It's spicy enough to keep me up all night."

"That's the way my dad liked it. Just go easy on the cayenne pepper," Sadie advised. "I grew up eating it that spicy, so I guess my body has gotten used to it."

"Have you tried that Boston clam chowder recipe I gave you?"

"Not yet," Sadie said with a smile, "but Sara is staying with me for a while, so I'm excited to make it for her. She loves seafood."

"Oh, good. Let me know how it turns out."

"Better yet, I'll invite you over for dinner one of these days."

Laura nodded. "I'll look forward to it. I plan to go out a lot more once this project is finished. I don't think I've ever worked for a more finicky client. He's asked me to change the font on the brochure four different times and keeps coming up with new ideas to add to the marketing campaign."

"Oh my," Sadie said. "Sounds like you have your hands full." Then she grinned. "Maybe you should send him some of my chili."

Laura laughed. "Oh, Sadie, don't tempt me! He contacts me day and night, so I could really use a break. And I know that chili would give me one."

"Just an idea," Sadie said playfully. "Anyway, I hope things slow down for you. It's been too long since we spent an afternoon together. Hank misses you and so do I."

"I'll be out to visit soon," Laura said, placing one arm over Sadie's shoulders and giving her an affectionate squeeze. "I promise."

"One large coffee, black," Hector announced, putting a steaming paper cup on the counter and nodding to Sadie. "And one cinnamon bun."

Sadie moved to pick it up. "I'll talk to you later, Laura."

"Sounds good, Sadie. See ya!"

Sadie carried her coffee and frosted cinnamon bun into the shop, her mouth already watering. After her restless night, she'd risen early for a morning hike and just eaten some yogurt and blueberries for breakfast. Now she was ready to kick off her workday with a delicious, fresh-baked cinnamon bun.

She set her coffee cup on the counter and then heard the door open behind her, setting off the bell. She turned to see Spike Harris enter the shop. He hesitated in the open doorway, his gaze on the cinnamon bun in her hand.

"Sorry," he said, "I thought you were open."

Sadie smiled. "You're right, Spike. The shop is open. I'm just enjoying a second breakfast." She held up the sweet bun in her hand. "Would you like to split it with me?"

"No, thanks, Sadie," he said, his brown leather cowboy boots thumping against the wood floor as he approached her. He wore faded blue jeans and a striped, red-and-white flannel shirt. "You go ahead and eat. I don't mind."

Sadie rounded the counter. "Well, I appreciate the company, but I don't want to keep you if you're in a hurry. Is there anything I can help you with?"

"No." Spike ran one hand through his shaggy, salt-and-pepper hair. He looked uncertain, as if he wasn't quite sure why he was there. "I didn't come here to buy anything."

"Well, that's just fine." Sadie hitched herself up on the stool and then took a sip of her latte. "Take all the time you want."

Spike scratched the silver stubble on his chin. As a musician, he often seemed more comfortable communicating with his music rather than his words. "I'm not here to look either."

Sadie decided her cinnamon bun could wait since Spike obviously had something on his mind. "So what brings you here?" she asked gently.

"Well, I saw something earlier," he began slowly, "and I thought I should tell you."

"Saw what?"

He cleared his throat. "It was a woman. She was behind your shop, really early this morning. The sun was barely up."

Sadie put down her cup, confused. "Behind my shop?"

He nodded. "I was driving by and saw her. It looked like she was throwing something over the fence into your backyard here."

"That's strange." She slid off the stool and headed for the back door of the shop.

Spike followed behind her as she opened the door and stepped outside. She kept a small patio set in the backyard during the warmer months of the year as well as some potted plants. At the moment, her purple mums were blooming.

Nothing looked out of place as Sadie's gaze scanned the yard. "Where exactly did you see this woman?" she asked Spike.

He pointed to the south side of her fence, where Sadie had planted some knockout rosebushes earlier in the year. She walked over to the bushes for a better look.

Then she saw it.

"I don't believe it," she breathed. She bent down and picked up the plastic bag that was now wedged between the fence and the bushes. Inside the plastic bag was a teddy bear—the same Steiff teddy bear that she'd sold to Giselle Fleur just the day before.

"What is this doing here?" she asked out loud.

Spike shrugged his broad shoulders. "I don't know. I had no idea she'd tossed over a stuffed animal. I wouldn't have bothered you about a kid's toy."

"Oh, Spike," she said, her hands gently clasping the plastic bag as she met his gaze. "This is so much more than a stuffed animal. It's a collector's item and quite valuable." She shuddered, imagining how awful the teddy bear's condition would have been if it had sat under a pile of snow during the winter months. "If you hadn't seen the woman, I might never have found it here until the spring."

He cracked a smile. "Then I'm glad I could help."

"Me too." Sadie thought about Giselle. "So this woman you saw by my fence, was she tall, with long, dark hair?"

Confusion swam in his blue eyes. "No, she was about medium-size for a woman. And I saw some blonde hair sticking out of the red baseball cap she wore."

Now it was Sadie's turn to be confused. "Well, that's even stranger." She wondered if someone had taken the teddy bear from Giselle. But if so, why return it to the Antique Mine in such an odd way? It made no sense.

"Let's get this teddy bear inside," Sadie said, heading back into the shop.

Spike followed her, closing the door behind him. "I haven't seen Alice in a while. How is she doing?"

"Just fine," Sadie said with a smile.

Spike couldn't hide the fact that he liked her daughter, and she could see a reddish blush suffuse his grizzled cheeks even now.

"Alice and Theo are off on some college tours for about the next ten days," she told him.

"Oh," he said, looking surprised, "well, I hope they have a good time."

"I'm sure they will." Sadie walked over to the front counter and carefully pulled the teddy bear out of the plastic bag. She looked at the button tag in its ear just to confirm that it was the same Steiff teddy bear that she'd purchased at the auction two days ago. The ID number matched and the year 1907 was stamped on the metal button, which meant it was the same bear.

She turned the bear over, noting that the loose stitches were still there. In fact, they appeared even looser than before. Some of the teddy bear's inner stuffing had even started to peek through.

"Well, I'd better get going," Spike said, shifting his weight from one foot to the other.

"Thanks again for stopping in," Sadie told him. "I really appreciate…" Her voice trailed off as the front door of the shop opened. She looked up, expecting to see Julie, who was scheduled to work today. Instead, she saw Officer Kyle Kenmore walk inside.

"Good morning," Kyle greeted them.

Spike turned around and gave a small nod in the officer's direction.

"Hello, Kyle." Sadie smiled, pleased and surprised that the police had landed on her doorstep before she'd even called them. "You've got great timing."

The young police officer walked toward the front counter, looking sharp and crisp in his neatly pressed uniform. Then his gaze fell on the Steiff teddy bear in Sadie's hands. "May I please see that teddy bear, Mrs. Speers?"

"Of course," Sadie held the bear out to him, assuming that Giselle had called the police as soon as she'd discovered the teddy bear was missing. But as Kyle grasped the teddy bear, something fell out through the loosely threaded, bottom torso seam.

A large, silver coin hit the hardwood floor with a resounding *clink* and then rolled in an uneven circle before falling flat. Officer Kenmore bent down to pick up the coin.

"Is that teddy bear some kind of bank?" Spike asked, his brow furrowed.

"No, it's just a very creative hiding place," Kyle said, looking grim as his gaze moved to Sadie. "Mrs. Speers, you're under arrest."

7

SADIE SAT FUMING IN THE STARK INTERVIEW ROOM OF THE Silver Peak Police Station. She couldn't believe she was here. And she really couldn't believe that it was Kyle Kenmore, a former student of hers at Silver Peak High, who had arrested her!

She'd tried to explain to him about the blonde woman throwing the teddy bear over the back fence of her shop. And Spike had backed up the story, telling Kyle that he'd witnessed the incident.

But Kyle wouldn't hear any of it. He'd been given orders to investigate and make an arrest if the Steiff teddy bear or any silver dollar coins were discovered. At least he hadn't placed her in handcuffs.

But how did the police know about the coin? And where had it come from? And why was it inside the Steiff teddy bear in the first place?

Those were questions that kept repeating themselves in Sadie's mind—questions that would have no answers until she was given some more information. She rubbed her hands together, chilled by the cool air in the room.

When Kyle had arrested her, Sadie had been so shocked that she hadn't even remembered to grab her fleece jacket. Now, an hour later, dappled sunlight streamed through one small, dusty window in the room and she could hear a tree swallow singing outside.

Sadie found it difficult to be cheerful in the hard, gray chair she sat on, the cold metal biting through her khaki slacks. She shifted on the seat, wondering if the police made this interview room purposefully uncomfortable so suspects would spill the beans faster. Only she didn't have any beans to spill, just lots of questions.

"Suspect," she said out loud, still shocked by the morning's turn of events.

She was a suspect!

That seemed so ridiculous that she wondered if this was some kind of practical joke. Or some kind of early birthday prank.

But her instincts told her this was all too real. One moment she'd been talking to Spike and the next moment she'd been arrested and carried away in the backseat of a police cruiser.

Spike had been livid on her behalf and she truly appreciated his defense of her. Before Kyle had carted her off, she'd asked Spike to contact Julie and tell her what had happened.

Spike had agreed, which meant that Julie probably knew the horrible story by now. She closed her eyes, a wave of embarrassment washing over her. No doubt people around town were already asking questions about her ride in the police cruiser. She'd seen Marge Ruxton standing in front of the bank across from the Antique Mine, her mouth agape as Officer Kenmore had driven off with Sadie safely ensconced in the backseat.

Sadie buried her face in her hands, fearing the story was spreading faster than a Colorado wildfire. She just hoped it was a fire that could be doused when the truth came out.

She tapped her foot impatiently on the gray linoleum floor, waiting for Sheriff Mac Slattery to enter the room. She'd been sitting in this chilly room for a good hour now and couldn't imagine what was keeping him. The sooner this misunderstanding got sorted out, the better.

Ten minutes later, the door opened and Sheriff Slattery walked inside. A big man, the sheriff filled the room with his presence. He carried the teddy bear and the silver coin, placing them in the center of the table. Then he pulled out the chair across from Sadie, the metal legs scraping against the floor in a way that made her teeth ache.

"Good morning, Sadie," the sheriff greeted her as he settled heavily into the chair. His dark hair was gray at the temples, and the deep lines in his face showed the physical wear and tear that working for the Denver Police Department for thirty years could bring. He and his wife, Anita, had moved to Silver Peak for a slower way of life, although they didn't socialize much in the community.

"Good morning, Mac," she said, relieved to finally see him. "Although it hasn't been a very good morning for me. I can't believe Kyle actually arrested me."

The sheriff sighed. "I'm afraid he didn't have a choice, Sadie. You were found with stolen property in your possession. We can't treat citizens here differently just because we know them and like them."

"I understand that," Sadie told him, making an effort to remain calm and resisting the urge to ask him for a sweater. "But this is simply nonsense. I had just found that teddy bear in the backyard of the Antique Mine when Kyle arrived. And how did he even know it was there?"

"We received a tip," the sheriff said.

"A tip? From whom?"

"The informant didn't give us a name, but they were adamant that we'd find the stolen property with you. I couldn't ignore it, Sadie, no matter how preposterous I thought it might be."

Sadie took a moment to let the information sink in. "When did this tip come in?"

"Yesterday evening. But I didn't want to disturb you at home, so we waited until today." He cleared his throat. "To be honest, I truly thought it was some kind of prank. I never expected that we'd find stolen property in your store."

That made her feel a tiny bit better. Now she could just tell him her side of the story and make this whole mess go away. "I bought that Steiff teddy bear at the Ferris estate auction in Breckenridge two days ago," she explained. "I had no idea it was stolen."

Sheriff Slattery pulled a notepad and a stubby pencil from his shirt pocket and began jotting down some notes that appeared barely legible to her. "Why don't you start there? Tell me everything that happened on the day you bought the teddy bear."

Sadie took a deep breath and gathered her thoughts, not wanting to forget anything important. Although she was certain that once the sheriff heard her story, he'd realize she was completely innocent.

She told him about attending the estate auction with Roz and her plan to buy the antique Victor Orthophonic phonograph. "Actually, I didn't even know about the Steiff teddy bear until it came up for bid," she said. "It was a last-minute addition to the auction and wasn't even listed in the catalog."

Sheriff Slattery arched a scraggly, gray brow. "Really? I've never attended an antique auction before. Is that kind of thing unusual?"

Sadie hesitated. "No, not really, especially when an auction is large enough to draw a lot of antique dealers, like that one. Consignment items are often added to the inventory since they'll usually bring in more money."

"So what made you interested in the old teddy bear?"

She found herself smiling at the question. "Steiff teddy bears are both cute and extremely collectible. They have a long history and are known to be high-quality items. I got quite a bargain on that Steiff bear too, although given what's happened today, I almost wish someone would have outbid me for it."

"Understandable," he said. "Did you know who else bid on the teddy bear?"

She shook her head. "No, I'm afraid not. Although I did ask for information about the owner of the teddy bear and was told that he—or she—wished to remain anonymous. Perhaps that person stole the bear or knows who did."

Sheriff Slattery met her gaze. "Why did you need to know the identity of the previous owner?"

"I didn't *need* to know it," she replied, and then realized she sounded a little defensive. Sadie softened her tone. "I just like to know how antiques are passed down through the years. Each one has a unique and often fascinating history."

She was about to expound more on the subject, but she saw the sheriff's brown eyes start to glaze over. Sadie knew she had a tendency to go on and on about antiques whenever she got started, but she also realized that her passion for them wasn't shared by everyone.

She paused for a long moment, aware that the sheriff was still staring at her. Was he waiting for her to say something incriminating? Or waiting for her to clear herself?

Either way, she could only tell him the truth and trust God to see her through this mess. "The point is," Sadie continued, "that the previous owner probably knows a lot more about this stolen property issue than I do. I suggest you find out his or her name and go from there."

One corner of the sheriff's mouth tipped up in a smile. "You can rest assured, Sadie, that I will do my level best to find out the identity of the original owner. However, the teddy bear wasn't stolen, as least as far as I know at this point. It was the silver coin inside the teddy bear that prompted the anonymous tipster to contact us."

She blinked. "Well, I certainly didn't know there was a coin inside of the teddy bear when I bid on it."

"And how much did you pay for the bear?"

She sat back in her chair, surprised that the interview was taking this long. Sheriff Slattery might be a little surly, but he seemed like a thorough and thoughtful police officer. That could only work in her favor. "Fourteen hundred dollars."

Mac's eyes popped. "Wow! That much for an old teddy bear?"

She smiled. "A very valuable, old teddy bear," she reminded him. "It's an original Steiff, made in 1907, and it's in excellent condition. Retail value starts around two thousand dollars for similar Steiff bears and that's a conservative estimate."

He leaned back in his chair, folding his beefy hands on top of his stomach. "So you did get a good deal. Any idea why it went for so low a price?"

Sadie shrugged. "It just happens that way sometimes. The opposite happens too. That Victor Orthophonic I wanted sold for a few hundred dollars over its appraised retail value."

He nodded, writing down some more notes on his pad. As the sound of his pencil scratching across the surface of the paper filled the silence, Sadie began thinking of some questions that she wanted to ask the sheriff.

"How do you know the silver coin inside the bear truly is stolen property," Sadie began, "especially since the tipster wouldn't give you his name or any other identifying information?"

"Because that silver coin matches the description of a coin taken in a recent theft in the area," the sheriff replied. "And we took a photograph of that coin and e-mailed the photo to the owner. He confirms that particular coin is part of his collection."

Collection. That word niggled something in her brain, and she remembered her lunch conversation with Alfred and Cecile. Then it hit her. "Brent Fielder," she said, meeting the sheriff's gaze. "There was a burglary at his mansion in Breckenridge a few weeks ago, right?"

"Yes, that's the one," he replied, arching a brow. "Have you ever met Mr. Fielder or been inside his home?"

Before Sadie could reply, the door to the interview room opened and Kyle stuck his head inside the door. "There's a lawyer here for Mrs. Speers."

"A lawyer?" Sadie echoed.

"He insists on seeing her immediately," Kyle told the sheriff.

"All right." Sheriff Slattery picked up his notepad and rose to his feet. "Send him in."

Kyle disappeared, leaving the door slightly ajar. Sheriff Slattery pushed his chair in. "I hope we can get this sorted out, Sadie. I really do."

"So do I," Sadie replied, watching him walk out of the room. She wondered who had sent her a lawyer and could only assume Julie or Spike had something to do with it.

While she waited, Sadie's gaze fell on the teddy bear and the silver coin. She hadn't seen them since Kyle had carted her away from the Antique Mine. Now they were obviously being held as evidence.

Sadie quickly pulled her cell phone out of her pocket and began taking pictures. She focused on the front of the coin, snapping a couple of photographs at close range so she could see every detail. The top of the coin had the words *E Pluribus Unum*, and the bottom of the coin had the date: 1904. Connecting the two points was a small circle of stars. And in the middle of the coin was the side profile of a woman's face; she wore a crown with the word *LIBERTY* printed on it.

Sadie turned the coin over, noting its heavy weight. The back of the coin had the image of an eagle on it, its wings lifted, as if ready to take flight. At the top of the coin were the words *United States of America*, and at the bottom, *One Dollar*, with a small star separating the two phrases on either side of the coin.

Sadie snapped two close-up shots of the back of the coin and then placed it in its original position on the table. Old coins and currency had never been her specialty, but she suddenly wanted to know all about them.

She glanced at the door, aware that the sheriff could return at any moment. For some reason, she didn't want him to catch her taking pictures of the evidence. She snapped a couple of pictures of the teddy bear. Then she placed the cell phone back in her pocket and slid into the folding chair, her heart pounding in her chest.

A moment later, the door opened and Edwin walked in. He smiled and said, "We've got to stop meeting like this."

Sadie laughed in spite of herself. "Well, you said you wanted to meet for lunch today. I thought we'd try someplace new." Despite her attempt at humor, she was both relieved and embarrassed for him to find her here.

"Do you have a dollar?" Edwin asked, closing the door behind him.

She blinked, confused. "I wasn't serious about lunch, Edwin."

His smile widened as he walked toward her and held out his hand. "I know, but I'm serious about needing a dollar."

Still confused, Sadie reached into her purse and pulled out her billfold. She plucked a dollar bill from inside the zippered pocket and handed it to him.

"Perfect," he said with a smile, taking it from her. "Now you've officially retained me as your attorney."

"You're the lawyer Kyle mentioned?"

"Well, I did pass the bar exam and worked as an attorney in Chicago before becoming a judge, so I still qualify."

His words made her chuckle. "Yes, I know you're a lawyer. I just didn't realize you were *my* lawyer. I had no idea when Kyle said my attorney was waiting to see me that it would actually be you."

"I guess it's your lucky day."

"I wouldn't exactly call it that," she said wryly. "I can't believe I'm here."

He knelt down by her chair. "I came as soon as I heard what happened."

Sadie swallowed a groan. "I was hoping you'd never hear about it at all. I suppose that means the news is all over town by now?"

"Well, this is Silver Peak," he said kindly. "But anyone who knows you will realize how ridiculous it was to arrest you."

She shook her head. "I still can't believe this is happening."

Edwin stood up and opened his arms. "Come here."

Sadie rose to her feet and closed her eyes as Edwin's arms came around her for a hug. She rested her head against his broad chest and inhaled the familiar scent of his aftershave.

"This is just what I needed," Sadie said, relaxing in his strong arms.

"Me too."

After a long moment, Sadie stepped away from him. "Are you sure I need a lawyer?"

He nodded. "Anyone who's arrested needs a lawyer." Edwin rounded the table and grabbed the chair that the sheriff had vacated. "I'm just lucky to get a client as pretty as you."

Sadie's cheeks grew warm, and she found herself wishing they actually were on their lunch date instead of sitting in the police station.

He sat down, his gaze landing on the silver coin and the teddy bear. "So that's the stolen property?"

"Yes. The coin was stolen," Sadie clarified, "not the teddy bear. That belongs to me—or Giselle—I'm not quite sure at this point."

"We can figure out the ownership of the teddy bear later," he said, scooting his chair closer to the table.

"How did you find out I was here?"

He smiled. "I called the shop to discuss our lunch date and Julie told me about your arrest. I simply couldn't believe it."

"That makes two of us. But I don't really need a lawyer, do I?" Sadie asked, still reeling from the events of this morning. "No one can possibly think I stole that silver coin."

"After all my years on the bench," he said slowly, his gaze intent on her face, "I believe anyone who is interviewed by the police, or the sheriff, should have a lawyer present. And it's not because the police aren't fair. I have the utmost respect for the men in blue. But the law is complicated, and things people say can be misunderstood or twisted in ways that they never meant."

Sadie shook her head. "Maybe that kind of thing happens in big cities like Chicago, but this is Silver Peak."

"And you've just been arrested," he gently reminded her. "Now, what did you and the sheriff talk about?"

"The Steiff teddy bear and how it came into my possession," Sadie told him. "Oh, and I did find out that the silver coin was stolen from Brent Fielder. He lives in Breckenridge and is one of the country's premier collectors."

Edwin gave a slow nod. "Yes, I've heard of the man and remember reading about the theft in the newspaper."

"He's known as the King of Fakes," Sadie told him, "since he collects fraudulent antiques that usually have a famous—or infamous—history behind them. But he does have several authentic collections, and I believe one of those is an extensive coin collection."

"So this coin could be real or fake?"

"I suppose so," Sadie mused, pausing for a long moment as she stared at the teddy bear and the coin. "Giselle must have been involved. Now it makes sense that she didn't want the teddy bear repaired and that she paid in cash. That way there would be no way to trace her."

"Giselle?"

Sadie told him about Giselle Fleur appearing in her shop yesterday, their conversation about the girl's dreams for a modeling career, and her impulsive decision to buy the bear.

"So this Giselle Fleur bought the Steiff teddy bear and paid cash for it?" Edwin said, his expression pensive.

"Yes. But apparently, some other woman tossed it into the backyard of the Antique Mine this morning," Sadie told him. "Spike saw her and described her to me as a medium-size blonde wearing a red baseball cap."

Edwin leaned forward. "Julie didn't give me all those details. Of course, as soon as I heard you were arrested, I came right over. So tell me more about this blonde woman."

Sadie shrugged. "There's not a lot more to tell. Apparently, Spike saw her while he was driving past the Antique Mine shortly after dawn. He couldn't tell from that distance what she was tossing over the fence." It occurred to her that Spike hadn't mentioned where the woman had gone after the teddy bear toss. Perhaps he hadn't stuck around long enough to find out or he'd simply lost sight of her.

"Did Spike recognize her?"

Sadie shook her head. "No, I don't think so." She met Edwin's steel blue gaze. "But who could she be? And why give the teddy bear back to me at all? It must be someone who knows Giselle. But why not sell it? The bear's worth over two thousand dollars."

Then another thought occurred to Sadie that made her stomach twist into a knot. "Maybe someone was trying to frame me for the Fielder theft. Giselle and the blonde woman might be the thieves themselves—and wanted to place that stolen coin in something from my shop. That could be why the police received the anonymous tip last night, and why Giselle didn't want me to repair the seam on the teddy bear."

Edwin listened as she explained that the anonymous caller had told the police they'd find the stolen property in Sadie's possession.

His brow furrowed. "Did the caller say the words 'stolen property' or did he specifically refer to the silver coin?"

"I don't know," she said slowly. "But he must have mentioned the coin, because Kyle arrested me as soon as the coin fell out of the teddy bear. And both he and the sheriff referred to the coin as contraband."

"The police are charging you with a class four felony, which means that silver coin is worth more than a thousand dollars but less than twenty thousand."

Her stomach dropped at the word *felony*.

Sadie stood up, hoping a little movement would make her feel better. "We need to find out if the police obtained a caller ID number for the anonymous tipster. That person must know something about the theft."

"It's doubtful the police have the phone number," Edwin said, shaking his head. "Otherwise, people wouldn't call in tips for fear of being found out."

"I guess you're right."

"Still, it wouldn't hurt to check. I'll ask Mac about it." Edwin rose from his chair. "Now, you and I still have a lunch date. So let me go see what I can do about getting you released."

She watched him walk to the door and then said, "Edwin, wait."

He turned around. "Yes?"

"You can't do this," she said softly, walking up to him. "You're the mayor of Silver Peak. How will it look if you're defending your girlfriend against this charge?"

He braced his hands gently on her shoulders and looked into her eyes. "I don't care about appearances," he said softly. "And anyone in this town who knows you is well aware that this charge is preposterous."

"But…"

He leaned closer to her. "No buts, Sadie. We need to get this matter in front of the magistrate so bail can be set before she leaves for the day."

"Bail?" Sadie exclaimed. "You can't be serious."

"Don't worry," he assured her, lowering his arms and reaching for the doorknob. "You've got a great reputation in this community. I'm sure, given all the circumstances, that you'll be released on your own recognizance."

"What exactly does that mean? Will I need to go in front of a judge or pay money to stay out of jail?"

He shook his head. "I'd be very surprised if either of those two things happen. The magistrate in this county is a fair woman and will handle the matter in her office. If you're released on your own recognizance, that means you won't have to pay anything."

A headache started to throb in her temple. She walked back to the table and sank into her chair. "I hope you're right."

"Just sit tight, Sadie," Edwin said with a tender smile. "This shouldn't take too long."

Then he was gone.

Sadie didn't like sitting still when there were things to be done. She didn't like feeling helpless either. It made her frustrated, angry, and a little scared.

"Heavenly Father," she prayed out loud. "Please help me through this. Help to open the eyes and minds and hearts of everyone involved in this mess."

She sucked in a deep breath, feeling a little bit stronger already. "And thank You, Lord, for bringing Edwin into my life." Her voice dropped to a whisper. "He means so much to me."

Sadie wondered what would have happened if Edwin hadn't shown up here today. She'd never even considered calling a lawyer, certain she could convince the sheriff of her innocence. But Sheriff Slattery had made it clear that his thoughts about the matter didn't mean as much as the evidence they had collected. Evidence that pointed directly at Sadie. She just hoped the sheriff would find the truth when he started to dig deeper.

And Sadie intended to do some digging herself. Someone was trying to frame her for a crime she didn't commit. But who? And why?

Sadie began to pace back and forth across the small interview room, planning a way to find answers to those questions so the real thief could be brought to justice.

8

"ARRESTED?" ALICE SQUEAKED OVER THE PHONE. "MOM, IS THIS a joke?"

Sadie sat in her living room later that evening, a fire blazing in the hearth, and Sara snuggled on the sofa with Hank. "I'm afraid it's no joke, Alice, but don't worry. Everything will be fine. Edwin is my lawyer and..."

"Lawyer?" Alice gasped. "You mean it's serious enough that you need a lawyer? Okay, I need to be there. Theo and I are catching the first flight out of Chicago tomorrow and..."

"No, you are not," Sadie said firmly. "This is all a big mistake, and Edwin and I are handling it. I just wanted to let you know in case anyone contacted you or Theo. You know how quickly news travels in Silver Peak."

"Oh, Mom," Alice said, sounding worried, "are you sure you don't need me there?"

"Honey, I'm positive." Sadie smiled over at Sara. "We've got everything handled here. Sara's doing her homework right now and I've got a busy week ahead. You two just enjoy the college tour and don't worry for a second about us."

Alice's long sigh carried over the line. "All right, but please promise you'll call me if you need anything—anything at all."

"I will," Sadie said, her heart filled with love for her daughter. The last thing she wanted was to put a damper on Alice and Theo's trip. "And I'll be just fine. This will probably all be settled by tomorrow, so don't you worry a bit."

Alice laughed. "Easier said than done, Mom."

"I know. At the very least, try to put your worry on hold until your trip is over."

"I'll do my best," Alice replied.

"Now, tell me about Theo's college visits."

Sadie settled back in her chair as she listened to the highlights of all the college tours. She stretched her legs out in front of her, relaxing for the first time all day. It had taken almost two hours for the magistrate to sign the papers releasing Sadie on her own recognizance.

The sheriff had kept the Steiff teddy bear and the silver coin as evidence, just as Sadie had assumed he would. After arriving home, she'd printed out the photographs she'd taken of both items.

"So Theo loved Northwestern," Alice said. "And I was so impressed with the campus, although Chicago is a more expensive place to live than Denver."

"Theo can always talk to Edwin about living in Chicago," Sadie told her. "He might have some good ideas about making it more affordable if Theo does choose Northwestern."

"Good idea," Alice replied, and then launched into a story about their tour of Michigan State.

Sadie enjoyed every word of their conversation, but eventually Alice had to end the call.

"So did Mom freak out about your arrest?" Sara asked as Sadie set her cell phone on the small table beside her.

"Only a little," Sadie said with a smile. "Alice said the two of you had a nice telephone chat before I came home."

"Kind of a boring call, actually." Sara ran her hand over Hank's head. The dog snuggled closer to the girl and flipped onto his back for a tummy rub. "We just talked about school and stuff. I didn't know you'd been put in jail."

"Nobody put me in jail," Sadie clarified. "I just talked to the sheriff about the teddy bear, and he's continuing his investigation. Like I told your mom, I'm sure it will all blow over soon."

The fire crackled as Sara stirred on the sofa, gently removing Hank's head from her lap. "Could I make some popcorn?"

"Sure, as long as you make enough for me too," Sadie said with a smile. "And how about some hot cocoa to go with it?"

"Yum," Sara said, rising off the sofa.

Sadie started to follow her, but Sara held up one hand. "Grandma, I can do it. I'm not a little girl anymore."

"I know." Sadie reached out to give her granddaughter a hug. In Sadie's heart, Sara would always be her little girl. "Okay, you go ahead and make us a snack. I want to do a little research."

Sara headed toward the kitchen and Hank quickly followed her—no doubt hoping to get a snack of his own.

Sadie breathed a sigh of contentment as she reached for her notebook on the coffee table. After the unsettling day she'd experienced, a peaceful evening at home was just the antidote she needed.

To her surprise, Sara had taken the news of her arrest in stride. Apparently, Sadie was the only grandmother in Sara's class who had ever been arrested. Even though that wasn't a mantle Sadie had ever wanted to wear, she was grateful that Sara didn't seem too upset about it.

Still, Sadie was determined to clear up the matter as soon as possible. Just the idea of this kind of suspicion hanging over her head made her uncomfortable. And the fact that Edwin had to come down to the police station to negotiate her release still made her cheeks warm with embarrassment.

She opened the notebook to the list she'd started shortly after her late-afternoon lunch with Edwin. She hadn't been able to eat a bite, but she enjoyed a cup of tea as Edwin explained how the legal process would work going forward. Apparently, the wheels of justice turned slowly, even in Silver Peak, but there was an evidentiary hearing scheduled a week from this coming Monday. That left Sadie about ten days to find the real culprit behind the crime.

At the top of her suspect list was Giselle Fleur. Giselle certainly hadn't portrayed herself as someone who could mastermind this kind of plot, but perhaps she was an actress as well as a model. Either way, Sadie was convinced the young woman was one of the keys to solving this mystery. Unfortunately, the only thing she knew about Giselle was her plan to travel to New York City to become a fashion model. Or was that part of the ruse?

Sadie retrieved her laptop from the office and carried it into the living room. The aroma of popcorn drifted through the air, making her mouth water. Sadie had made Laura's recipe for Boston clam chowder for supper, but she hadn't been hungry herself. Now that she was finally taking some positive action, her appetite was starting to return.

Sliding back into her chair, Sadie opened the laptop and turned it on. After it warmed up, she typed the words *Giselle Fleur Colorado* into the Internet search engine. Links appeared on the screen, but none of them matched her search. Then she tried looking for Giselle Fleur on Facebook. She found one match for that name, but that Giselle Fleur lived in Ghana, Africa, and looked nothing like the woman who had appeared in the Antique Mine yesterday.

Not ready to give up, Sadie looked at Web sites for local modeling agencies in the Breckenridge, Denver, and Colorado Springs areas. She was scrolling through the photographs of models on the first Web site when Sara walked into the room carrying two cups of hot cocoa.

"Here you go, Grandma," she said, handing one of the cups to Sadie. Sara set the other cup on the coffee table and then made a second trip to the kitchen to retrieve a big bowl of buttered popcorn, along with two smaller empty bowls.

"Looks like there's plenty for both us," Sadie said with a smile as Sara set the big bowl on the coffee table. She'd smothered the popcorn in butter and brought the salt shaker with her so they could each season their own portion.

"If there's any left over, I'm going to eat it for breakfast tomorrow." Sara scooped up a bowl of popcorn for each of them before plopping down on the sofa. "Have you ever had popcorn with milk, Grandma? It tastes like buttery cereal."

"No, but I might give it a try," she said, feeling adventurous. She sprinkled some salt on her popcorn and then took a sip of her hot cocoa. "My, this is good."

Sara flashed a smile. "Thanks. The trick is to put a little salt in it. Mia's grandma does that all the time."

"I'll have to remember that," Sadie said before taking another sip. Then she turned her attention back to the modeling Web site on her laptop screen.

The two of them sat in a comfortable silence, Sadie on her laptop and Sara texting on her cell phone, while Hank snored on the braided rug in front of the fireplace.

Sadie scrolled through the photos on the modeling Web sites, hoping to find one that resembled Giselle. She was convinced now that the young woman hadn't given Sadie her real name. Giselle may have even lied about her dream of pursuing a modeling career too, although Sadie's instincts told her otherwise. She'd seen the passion in Giselle's brown eyes when she'd spoken about her dream of moving to New York to advance her career.

But why would Giselle involve herself in framing Sadie if she wanted to be a fashion model? Sadie was still missing too many pieces of this puzzle, and she wasn't sure where to look next.

Sadie had just finished her third bowl of popcorn when she heard Sara groan. She looked up from her laptop. "What's wrong?"

"There's a new post up on the *Chatterbox*, Grandma," Sara said, referring to Silver Peak's local social blog. The author of the blog remained anonymous, intriguing residents and maintaining an uncanny ability to keep up with all the latest news and gossip around town.

"Oh boy…," Sadie said.

"Yep. It's about the teddy bear. And you."

Sadie knew she shouldn't be surprised, but the fact that the *Chatterbox* had a post up about her arrest only a few hours after it had happened told her how quickly the news had spread.

"Why don't you read it to me?" Sadie suggested, curious to hear what the *Chatterbox* had to say.

"Are you sure? The title of the blog post is 'Fuzzy Wuzzy Funny Business.'"

"I can bear it," Sadie said, smiling at her own pun. "And you have to admit, that's a pretty clever title, even if it is about me."

Sara giggled, and then cleared her throat and began to read the rest of the blog post out loud.

"Did a warm, cuddly teddy bear land everyone's favorite Antique Lady in hot water with the Silver Peak PD? They gave her a ride to the station for a cozy chat with the big chief. He's not talking, but word around town is that a teddy bear made a crash landing in the Antique Mine's backyard and started all the fuss. Throw in a mysterious blonde woman, a silver coin, and a mayor with a conflict of interest, and you've got trouble in Toyland."

"Well, I guess the news is out," Sadie said after Sara finished reading. She wondered how the *Chatterbox* knew so much. But maybe that was a good thing. Perhaps other people had seen the blonde woman outside her shop this morning and had recognized her.

"What does it mean," Sara said slowly, "about the mayor with a conflict of interest?"

Sadie swallowed a sigh. "Edwin came to the police station today to act as my attorney."

Sara's eyes widened with apprehension. "You mean, it's bad enough that you need a lawyer?"

"No, dear, it's just a precaution," Sadie said gently. "Edwin's spent decades in the legal profession and he thinks it wiser to have a lawyer than not to have one. Don't worry, everything will be all right."

Sadie's frustration with this mess was compounded by the fact that people she cared about were affected by it too. She hated to possibly put Edwin on the hot seat with his constituents. Sadie knew most wouldn't care, but there were always a few malcontents who liked to stir the pot.

"I hope you're right, Grandma," Sara said. Then she got up from the sofa. "I'm going upstairs to study some more. We have a big English test tomorrow."

"Okay," Sadie said, as Sara walked over to give her a hug. "Don't stay up too late. And let me know if you need any help."

"I will." Sara headed upstairs with Hank trailing behind her, leaving Sadie alone in the living room.

The fire crackled and snapped in the hearth, keeping the large living room cozy and toasty warm. Sadie tucked her legs underneath her as she turned back to her laptop. So far her search for Giselle was going nowhere.

Maybe I started in the wrong place, Sadie thought to herself. She walked over to the bookshelf and scanned the books until she found one that she knew had information about old coins. She carried it back to the sofa and began flipping through the pages as she settled into the soft cushions.

After searching for a few minutes, she saw a picture that looked almost identical to the silver coin that had dropped out of the teddy bear.

"The Morgan silver dollar was produced in the late nineteenth century and the early twentieth century," Sadie read out loud. "Specifically, between the years of 1878 and 1904. It was also produced in the year 1921, the only time the coin was minted in Denver."

Her gaze slowly scanned the page, not wanting to miss anything important. She learned that it was composed of 90 percent silver and 10 percent copper, and weighed 26.73 grams.

Curious, Sadie picked up her laptop and searched for the value of a 1904 Morgan silver dollar in good condition. When the price appeared on the screen, she frowned. "That can't be right."

The price quoted was below one hundred dollars. She checked other coin Web sites and found prices ranging from fifty to eighty dollars. The police were charging her with a class four felony, stating the value of the coin was over one thousand dollars. That simply didn't make sense. Had Brent Fielder inflated the value of his coin after the theft—or was there something else going on?

She turned back to the book to read more about the Morgan silver dollars. "The coin was named after George Morgan, a mint assistant engraver for the United States. Each coin is marked with a letter to represent the city where it had been minted."

Sadie got up from the sofa and retrieved the photograph she'd printed out earlier. She could see the letter *D* on the coin, just below the eagle, which she knew meant that it had been minted in Denver.

But then that conflicted with something she'd just read. According to the book, 1921 was the only year the Morgan silver dollars had been minted in Denver. So either the book was wrong—or the coin was wrong.

The King of Fakes.

Could it be possible that the coin was counterfeit? Sadie grabbed her laptop computer again and typed the words *Morgan silver dollar* and *Brent Fielder* into the search engine.

A moment later, a link appeared to a five-year-old column in an online magazine called *Coin Collectors Quarterly.*

"Here it is," Sadie said out loud. "Brent Fielder recently purchased all ten of the infamous Huntley coins. Forged to resemble Morgan silver dollars, the Huntley coins were almost identical to the real thing. According to reliable sources, the total purchase price for all ten Huntley coins topped twelve thousand dollars."

Sadie leaned back on the sofa and set the laptop aside. Now she knew why the police had charged her with a felony. She just hoped she could find a way to point them in the direction of the real culprit.

9

—————

THE NEXT MORNING, SADIE HAD JUST OPENED THE SHOP WHEN Harry Polmiller walked through the door holding a brown paper sack in his hand.

"Good morning, Harry," she said, greeting him with a smile.

At ninety-four years old, Harry still had the stamina of a man twenty years his junior. The oldest congregant at Campfire Chapel, Harry had been a fixture in Silver Peak for as long as Sadie could remember.

"Good morning, Sadie." Harry walked toward her and set the bag on the counter with a resounding *clunk*. "Fine day, isn't it?"

"It sure is." Then she pointed to the bag. "What do you have there?"

He grimaced. "I'm not sure if it's trash or treasure. To be honest, I tossed it into the Dumpster last night, ready to be rid of the thing once and for all. But this morning, I dug it out again. I figured you could tell me whether it's worth keeping."

Intrigued, Sadie opened the bag and pulled out an ugly black platter that sported two dents and a threadlike scratch down the middle. The scratch revealed the silver that lay underneath the black surface. "Well," she said slowly, "this is interesting."

He chuckled. "I suppose that's one word for it."

"Tell me about this platter," she said, smoothing one hand over the tarnished surface. She loved the feel of the metal against her palm, and the weight of the platter revealed its high quality.

"Well," Harry began, scratching his chin, "it's been in my family for as long as I can remember. I think it was made by one of the local silversmiths around here. Anyway, Grandma Polmiller used to serve fancy little cakes on it whenever guests stopped by." He gave Sadie a wry smile. "Not that us grandkids counted as guests. She kept a big jar of cookies in the kitchen for us. Funny how that jar was never empty, considering she had grandkids underfoot almost every day of the year."

Sadie smiled. "Sounds like heaven to this grandma." She picked up the tray and flipped it over to examine the bottom, hoping to see the mark of the silversmith who had forged it, but the black tarnish covering the surface made that impossible.

"Do you think it's worth saving?" Harry asked. "I wanted to give it to my daughter, but not in the condition it's in now."

"Oh, it's definitely worth saving," she told him. "Let me see what I can do with it. It may take me a while."

"No hurry," he said, waving off any concern. "No hurry at all. I know you're busy."

For a moment, Sadie wondered if Harry was referring to her recent arrest. She studied his face, but his clear blue eyes met hers with an innocence that told Sadie that he hadn't heard the latest gossip in town.

She breathed a deep sigh of relief, grateful that she didn't have to talk about it at this moment. Right now, the only thing that mattered was the piece of history in front of her. She picked up the tarnished tray, eager to start working on it. "I'll give you a call when it's done."

"That's fine," Harry told her. "And don't worry if it's a lost cause. It almost ended up in the trash once. I'm sure it can find its way back there again."

"I don't believe in lost causes," she said with a smile.

"Well, good luck, then," he said, chuckling as he headed out of the shop. "Have a good day, Sadie."

"You too," she called after him and turned toward the back room. She carried the tray there and set it at her workstation, moving a polishing cloth out of the way and flipping on the desk light so she could take a better look.

A moment later, the bell above the shop door sounded, signaling the arrival of another customer. She stepped out of the back room to see Roz marching toward her.

"We need to make an enemies list," Roz announced, placing her large purple handbag on the front counter.

Sadie smiled at Roz's stern expression. She'd called her yesterday, shortly after leaving the police station, and let her know about the arrest and everything that had happened in between. "I assume you've read the *Chatterbox*?"

"Trouble in Toyland?" Roz said with a disdainful sniff. "How silly is that?"

"Very silly, although I have to admit it does have a nice ring to it."

Roz's expression softened and she even laughed a little. "Okay, it does. And if you weren't involved, I might not be so upset. But I still can't believe you were arrested. That's simply insane!"

"It sure doesn't seem real." Sadie looked around the shop, wondering if she'd have many customers today. Would people stay away after her arrest or come inside to satisfy their curiosity and try to get the full scoop?

"You know," Sadie continued, "Julie offered to work for the next few days until this gets sorted out. I might just take her up on it."

"You should," Roz said without hesitation. "The faster you nip this nonsense in the bud, the better." She pulled a sheet of lined notepaper out of her handbag. "That's why I suggested making an enemies list. It seems like someone's out to get you."

Sadie glanced at her paper. "Looks like you've already written down a name."

"The Marleys," Roz said. "They've been feuding with your family for decades."

Roz was right, at least about some of the Marleys, but Sadie didn't want to accuse one of them without any proof. "But things have been fairly quiet lately. Why would they do something like this now? It just seems too mean-spirited, even for some of them."

"I don't think we should eliminate anyone yet." Roz picked up a pencil off the counter. "So who else should we add?"

Sadie thought for a long moment. "I honestly can't think of anyone."

"What about that Herbert fellow at the auction? You said it was strange that he didn't attempt to bid on the Steiff teddy bear. Maybe there was a reason." Roz leaned forward, her eyes narrowing. "Maybe he knew about the silver coin in the teddy bear and called in that anonymous tip."

Sadie considered the possibility. "You may be right, although Herbert never struck me as the criminal type."

"I'm writing his name down anyway," Roz said. "We have to start somewhere."

"I agree," Sadie told her. "I've been focusing on Giselle Fleur, if that's really her name. But so far I've come up empty. So add her to the list too. In fact, let's forget about an enemies list, and just call it a contact list. I'm going to talk to every person who I know had contact with that teddy bear. One of them had to have placed that coin inside."

"*Enemies list* has a better ring to it," Roz said with a impish smile. "But I guess we can change it to a contact list." Then she jotted the name *Giselle Fleur* on to the list.

Sadie tapped one finger on the marble countertop, thinking about the Ferris estate auction. She'd asked Starla for the name of the Steiff teddy bear's owner, but was told that information was confidential. Still, circumstances had changed since that conversation. Now it wasn't curiosity that drove Sadie's need to know the identity of previous owner, but her very freedom.

"Write down *Marvin Burton* and *Starla Burton*," Sadie told Roz. "I need the name of the teddy bear's original owner. Then I can track down everyone who had access to the teddy bear from the time it left the owner's hands until I picked it up at the auction."

"Marvin and Starla Burton," Roz said, her head bent over the list. "Got it."

"And Brent Fielder. It's his coin, after all. His *counterfeit* coin." Roz blinked. "Counterfeit? What do you mean?"

Sadie told her about the research she'd done last night and the discovery that no 1904 Morgan silver dollar had ever been minted in Denver. "I called the Denver mint this morning just to make certain and they confirmed what I'd read in the book."

"Well, isn't that something?" Roz said as she jotted down the name *Brent Fielder* on her list.

"That's all I can come up with for now," Sadie said, certain she'd think of more names later. "It's a start anyway."

Roz pushed the list toward Sadie. "Now, tell me what I can do to help."

Sadie gave her a wistful smile. "I don't suppose you can stop the rumor mill for me."

"I'm doing my best." Roz sighed. "I had a run-in with Marge Ruxton at the Market this morning. I overheard her telling the cashier that she always thought you'd overcharged for your antique restoration services."

Sadie had done some of her best work restoring antiques for Marge, but the woman didn't like to part with her money and had often bickered with Sadie about the cost.

"So I let them both know that you were innocent," Roz continued.

Sadie laughed. "I can always count on you to stand up for me."

"Always," Roz said with a nod. "You're not guilty of anything, Sadie. We both know that. Soon, everyone else in town will know it too."

The words made Sadie's throat tighten and she gave a nod. "Thanks for coming to my defense, Roz."

Roz's expression softened. "Anytime, Sadie. It's just so silly. I hate that you have to deal with it."

Sadie squared her shoulders. "Well, I'm not going to let it consume my life. I have a shop to run."

"Then I'll get out of your hair," Roz said cheerfully. "Oh, I almost forgot. I brought you that DVD you wanted to borrow." She fished the *Maltese Falcon* DVD out of her purse and set it on the counter. "Call me if you need anything."

"Thanks, I will," Sadie promised, watching her best friend walk out the door. Then she placed the DVD in a drawer and looked around the shop, ready for some time with her antiques. She walked to the back room and approached her worktable, positioning the platter under the best light.

The heavily tarnished handles on each side of the platter were ornate, with finely detailed scrollwork that was continued around the edges of the platter. Tarnish on silver plating looked downright ugly and certainly not like anything you'd want to serve food on. However, Sadie knew that with the proper materials and lots of elbow grease she could restore Harry's platter to its status as a treasured family heirloom.

Sadie turned the platter over, deciding to start on the back of it first. She pulled a clean cotton cloth from a drawer and then dampened it with cool water, aware that hot water could damage some silver surfaces. Then she squeezed a gumball-size drop of silver polish on to the cloth and began rubbing it over the center of the platter in a small, circular motion.

Too many people she knew gave up on polishing silver, often frustrated by the hard-to-reach tiny grooves and crevices found in the handles or etched designs. She'd learned that patience was the key, and as she worked, the black tarnish began to fade and the glimmer of shiny silver peeked through. The spot she'd worked on was only about the size of a quarter, but it promised to reveal a lovely patina underneath. To her delight, she could now see the maker's mark, which was in the shape of a hunter's bow.

She thought of the memories this silver tray had made for Harry and his loved ones and how many times his grandmother must have polished this platter just as Sadie was doing now. He might be tickled to find out the name of the silversmith who had actually made the platter. Perhaps the silversmith was even related to the Polmiller family. She made a mental note to look into it later.

Then Sadie smiled to herself, thinking of that full cookie jar in Grandma Polmiller's kitchen and how that memory had brightened Harry's eyes, even after all these years.

Removing the tarnish from the platter would require days, not merely hours, of work, but once it was done, Sadie would be better able to evaluate the dents and scratches marring the silver. For now, she was content to rub the cloth in small circles, the process soothing to her.

"I come to the garden alone," she sang softly as she worked, "while the dew is still on the roses. And the voice I hear, falling on my ear, the Son of God discloses." She squeezed another dab of silver polish on the cloth and started working on a new spot. "And He walks with me, and He talks with me, and He tells me I am His own..."

The serenity of the moment and the song in her heart made all her troubles temporarily fall away. "And the joy we share as we tarry there, none other has ever known."

But even as the lyrics soothed her, Sadie feared, deep down, that her troubles were just beginning.

10

THE NEXT DAY, SADIE LEFT THE ANTIQUE MINE IN JULIE'S capable hands and drove to Breckenridge to start digging. She had photos of the teddy bear and the silver coin with her, along with some questions that she wanted to ask auctioneer Marvin Burton.

In her mind, he was one of the prime suspects in this mess. *Someone* had placed that Huntley coin inside the teddy bear.

According to the sheriff, the coin had been among ten Huntley coins stolen from a collection belonging to Brent Fielder. Was it possible that the teddy bear had been used to conceal one of the Huntley coins and then purchased from her to retrieve it?

But why?

Sadie nibbled her lower lip as she drove, trying to work it out in her mind. Last night, she'd even written down the possible steps the thief had taken:

1. Steal the ten Huntley coins from the Fielder mansion.
2. Hide one Huntley coin in the Steiff teddy bear.
3. Sell the teddy bear anonymously at the Ferris auction.
4. Track the buyer of the teddy bear and buy it back.

That's where she'd gotten stuck. Because in that scenario, the person who'd bought the bear from her, Giselle, would have taken the silver coin out of the teddy bear. Unless Giselle had put it in the teddy bear after purchasing it from her and then made the anonymous call to the police, hoping to frame Sadie.

And, if so, Giselle had been working with the blonde woman who had tossed the Steiff teddy bear in the backyard of her shop.

That didn't make a lot of sense to Sadie either. Unless, this was some type of fencing operation where the thief was using the auction service to move the stolen property to potential buyers. If so, could Marvin be aware of it? And why had the conspirators in this fencing operation allowed her to outbid them for the teddy bear? Wouldn't someone who was in on the scam bid high enough to win the teddy bear?

Had it simply been a mistake to let Sadie win the bear? A mistake that Giselle had rectified by shelling out twenty-four hundred dollars to get it back?

The more she tried to figure it out, the more confused she became. The coin itself might not even be worth twenty-four hundred. So why give the bear back, since it was worth at least that much?

Sadie knew she needed more information. She tried to remember the faces of the other bidders for the teddy bear, but they blurred with the faces of hundreds of bidders at countless auctions she'd attended over the decades.

And even if she could remember their faces, she didn't know their names. She supposed there was a chance she'd run into one of them again at another auction, but there were dozens of auctions every day across Colorado. There was no way she could attend each one looking for the people who had bid against her for the Steiff bear.

She took a deep breath and then slowly released it as she drove along the winding highway leading to Breckenridge. Towering aspen trees bordered both sides of the road. Soon their green leaves would turn gold and orange, setting the mountains ablaze with the colors of autumn.

"Maybe Marv isn't the best place to start," she murmured out loud, thinking of another man who might have some answers. As she reached the city limits of Breckenridge, she made a right-hand turn and headed for Colorado Mountain College.

Fifteen minutes later, she walked into Bates Hall on the college campus. It was almost noon, which made it the perfect time to ask Alfred out for lunch so she could pick his brain. She'd often popped in over the years with impromptu lunch invitations and Alfred had always been happy to see her. Sometimes Cecile joined them for lunch if her schedule allowed.

The door to Alfred's office stood open and she saw him seated behind his desk, an open lunch pail in front of him. He looked as dapper as always, in his gray pin-striped suit, white dress shirt, and navy blue bow tie.

"Hello," she greeted him, standing in the open doorway. "I came here to invite you to lunch, but it looks like you beat me to it."

He dabbed at his mouth with a paper napkin, and then put down the sandwich in his hand. "Sadie, this is a nice surprise!"

Alfred stood up, a smile creasing his face. "Please, come in and sit down."

"Don't let me interrupt your lunch," Sadie said, walking to the chair nearest his desk and taking a seat. "I don't mind if you eat in front of me."

"No worries, I was finished." He wrapped the sandwich in a napkin and then closed it inside the lunch box. "What brings you to town?"

"Questions," she said simply.

A twinkle of curiosity gleamed in Alfred's eyes. "Now, that sounds intriguing." He checked his watch. "Unfortunately, I have to be at a meeting soon, but we can talk for a few minutes if you'd like."

Sadie wished she could have longer than a few minutes to lay out the whole situation, but that's what she probably deserved for dropping in unannounced. For a moment, she considered postponing the conversation and inviting Alfred and Cecile to supper instead, but since Sara was staying with her, Sadie knew that wouldn't work.

"Any time you can spare will be helpful," she said, digging the photographs of the Huntley coin out of her purse. "I'd like to know what you can tell me, if anything, about this coin."

Alfred took the pictures from her and studied them, his glasses now balanced on the tip of his nose.

She'd printed off some additional photographs this morning while Sara had been eating her breakfast of chocolate waffles with whipped cream and strawberries. Sadie loved cooking for her granddaughter and making special treats. She couldn't resist eating some chocolate waffles herself, and while they might not be good for her waistline, the time Sadie spent in the kitchen with Sara made her heart happy.

"Interesting," Alfred mused, his gaze on the photographs in his hand. "It's old, that's for sure. The date's a little faded, but it looks like 1904 to me."

"Me too," Sadie said.

"Do you know anything about this coin?"

"I believe it was minted by a man named Huntley." Sadie waited for Alfred's reaction and wasn't disappointed.

"This is one of the Huntley counterfeit coins?" He took another look at the photograph. "Well, what you do know! This is from the Brent Fielder collection, right? I heard the Huntley coins had been among the stolen items." Then Alfred's white eyebrows popped up as he turned to meet her gaze. "Wait, how can you have photographs of one of the stolen coins?"

"It's a long story," Sadie said, not sure that they had time to go into it even if she wanted to. "But it starts with the Ferris estate auction that took place here in Breckenridge three days ago."

He nodded. "I wanted to be there, given the history of the Ferris family in this town. Did you come away with any good buys?"

"Actually, I did." Sadie pulled the photographs of the Steiff teddy bear from her purse and set them on the desk in front of Alfred. "I won a 1907 Steiff teddy bear in excellent condition. You know the value of these bears since you have one yourself."

"I do, indeed," he said, leaning in for a long look. "The Ferris family owned so many valuable antiques and collectibles."

"Oh, this teddy bear wasn't part of the Ferris estate," Sadie clarified. "It was put up for sale by an anonymous seller."

"So what does this teddy bear have to do with the Huntley coin?" he asked, shifting in his chair.

Sadie opened her mouth to tell him, but the sound of footsteps behind her made her turn around instead.

A young woman appeared in the doorway, wearing blue jeans, a pink polo shirt, and a pair of white tennis shoes with pink laces. Her wavy, brown hair hung just above her shoulders.

"Oh, hello," the young woman said with a shy smile as she looked from Alfred to Sadie and then back again. "Is this a bad time?"

"No, Val," Alfred said, waving her in. "Sadie, this is my graduate teaching assistant this semester, Valerie Nichols. Val, this is Sadie Speers, a good friend of mine and quite the historian in her own right."

"Nice to meet you," Sadie said to Valerie, reaching out to shake her hand. "How are you enjoying your assistantship?"

"It's great," Val exclaimed. "Professor Daly is awesome. I learn something new every day."

"He is awesome," Sadie agreed.

Alfred chuckled. "I'll have to tell Cecile I'm too awesome to clean out the rain gutters this weekend and see how that goes over."

Sadie laughed. "Just tell her she's all wet."

Alfred laughed along with her as Val looked between them. Then the sound of a clock chimed in the office.

"Oops," Alfred said, reaching for the cell phone on his desk. "That's my alarm." He turned off the alarm and then rose from his chair. "I hate to chat and run, but I'd better get going."

"I understand," Sadie said, feeling a tiny stab of disappointment that they couldn't visit longer.

Alfred picked up the photographs of the Huntley coin. "Why don't I have Val make a copy of the coin pictures so I can study them when I have more time? Then I can e-mail you with anything I discover."

Before Sadie could reply, Val, who had been hovering in the doorway, moved farther into the office. "I'll make the copies right away," she said, taking them from Alfred. "The college has a great color laser printer that makes perfect copies."

"You can just keep those," Sadie told them. "I have extras and the pictures on my computer, so if I need more copies I'll just print them out."

"Are you sure?" Alfred asked.

"Positive." Sadie rose from her chair. "It was nice to meet you, Val."

"You too, Ms. Speers," Val replied, already moving to straighten up the area around Alfred's desk.

"Please call me Sadie." Then she turned and walked with Alfred out of the office and into the bustling hallway. "I sure had fun at lunch the other day. Let's get together again soon."

"Sounds good to me," he said. "I'll tell Cecile to give you a call, although it seems her schedule is even more packed than mine these days."

"We'll just have to find a time to make it work." Then she smiled. "I'd better skedaddle so you can get to your meeting."

"Okay, see you soon." Alfred gave her a wave as they parted ways.

Sadie stood in the hallway for a long moment and watched him hurry toward one of the classrooms. He was a popular professor at the college, and more than one student greeted him as he made a dash to his destination. Then she squared her shoulders and turned toward the door.

She had an important destination of her own.

After Sadie left the college campus, she headed straight for the office of Burton & Best Auction Services. She'd called ahead to make sure Marvin was in the office today and not out auctioneering.

The office was located on the outskirts of Breckenridge, and Sadie followed the directions she'd written down at home this morning. But she was surprised to find herself leaving the paved streets of the city behind and driving on a gravel mountain road. Towering pine trees on either side of the road made Sadie wonder if the directions she'd found on the Internet had been wrong.

She glimpsed a small herd of longhorn sheep in a clearing ahead and slowed the car. They looked up as she approached and just stared as she passed the grassy incline where they stood grazing.

·She was about to turn the Tahoe around and head back to Breckenridge when she saw a thin curl of white chimney smoke about a mile ahead. If nothing else, she could stop and ask for directions, Sadie told herself.

When she crested the hill she saw a log cabin in the distance with a stone chimney. That was the source of the smoke, and a sign posted on the wide front porch told Sadie that she'd reached her destination.

The white, hand-painted words on the pine-green sign looked slightly off center and read: *Burton Auction Services*. It was apparent to Sadie that the sign had once read *Burton & Best Auction Services*, but someone had painted over part of it to erase the thirty-year partnership between Marvin and Leo.

A dog began to bark as she pulled into the white gravel driveway, and a moment later she saw an Irish setter round the back of the log cabin and approach her car. The dog began to wag its tail as Sadie climbed out of her Tahoe, and she smiled as she bent down to pet it.

"Hello there" she said, her hand caressing the dog's silky red fur.

The dog followed her up the steps of the wooden porch and walked over to a woven straw rug and sat down on it. Sadie took a moment to admire the two hand-crafted chairs constructed from tree stumps and artfully entwined tree branches. Another stump stood between them, serving as a small table. Several coats of clear varnish had been applied to the top of the table stump, its brown and white rings showing the long life of the tree.

Sadie walked over to the wide front door and turned the brass knob. It opened easily, the gentle squeak of the hinges announcing her arrival. She walked inside, expecting to see the same rustic interior that she'd found on the front porch. To her surprise, the furniture and decor were much more eclectic.

The log walls of the large reception area were filled with framed vintage movie posters. There were several Alfred Hitchcock movies represented, including *North by Northwest* and *Rear Window*. A bright orange *Vertigo* poster hung above the white stone fireplace, the color matching the low flames in the hearth. Sadie appreciated the warm, cozy room on this crisp day and unzipped her purple North Face vest as she walked toward the reception desk. No one sat in the black leather chair behind the desk, although classical music emanated from a pair of computer speakers.

A small brass elephant sat on the black quartz countertop, along with a fabric pumpkin basket filled with butterscotch candies. Sadie helped herself to one of the candies, wondering if anyone had heard her enter. After a few moments, she tapped the bell on the counter, the sound reverberating in the room.

Marv emerged from the back hallway, his bulky frame moving quickly into the room. He wore faded blue jeans and a green-and-white-checked shirt with the sleeves pushed up to the elbows, revealing hairy tanned forearms. His face was tan too, although the top half of his forehead was as white as snow where his cowboy hat usually sat.

"Hello, Sadie," Marvin greeted her. "How long have you been standing out here?"

"Not long," she said with a smile. "I've just been admiring all your movie posters." Her gaze moved around the room. "What a fun collection."

He grinned. "Starla is the classic movie lover in the family, although she's converted me into a Hitchcock fan. I like Jimmy Stewart movies too." He pointed to the poster of Jimmy Stewart hoisting a young Donna Reed into the air. "*It's a Wonderful Life* is Starla's favorite movie and her favorite poster."

"I like that movie too," Sadie told him. "I've never been to your office before. I didn't realize it was in such a lovely log cabin."

"This cabin has been in my family for years," Marvin explained, "and it's one of my favorite places in the world, so I decided to spend my working hours here too."

"Smart plan," she said, placing the candy wrapper in the front pocket of her khaki slacks. "I met your dog outside. He's such a sweetie."

Marvin grinned. "Rufus isn't much of a guard dog, as you could probably tell, but he's part of the family."

"I know what you mean. I have a furry family member of my own." She realized she was putting off the conversation she wanted to have with Marvin. They'd known each other a long time and she didn't want to do anything to create a rift between them. But she simply didn't have any other choice.

"So what brings you here today, Sadie?" Marvin asked, a twinkle in his green eyes. "Hoping for an early peek at the Summit County sale catalog?"

The Summit County sale was an annual event that brought in consignment items from all around the state. The two-day auction included an arts-and-crafts fair and musical entertainment. Something told her that when Marvin discovered the real reason for her visit, any sneak peeks would probably be out of the question.

"Actually, I'm here about the Ferris auction," she began.

He leaned one forearm on the counter. "Oh?"

"Do you remember that teddy bear I bought?"

"The Steiff?" He gave a slow nod. "I sure do. Not having second thoughts, are you?"

That was a loaded question. If she'd known the trouble the teddy bear would bring into her life, she probably would have kept her mouth firmly closed during the bidding. But it was too late for regrets now. Besides, the teddy bear wasn't to blame—it was whoever had put that stolen Huntley coin inside the teddy bear.

"Not exactly second thoughts," she replied and then pointed to the cozy sitting area next to the fireplace. "Do you mind if we sit down?"

His eyebrows hitched up a notch, but he nodded in agreement. "Sure. Can I get you something to drink first? I believe Starla brewed a pot of hot coffee before she left to do some shopping. I like it strong and black, but we have some cream on hand if you like it lighter."

Sadie followed him over to the fireplace. "I'd love some coffee. Black, please."

Marvin fetched a cup for her as Sadie took a seat on the black leather sofa. Then he sat down in a matching armchair opposite her.

"Something tells me this is serious," he said, searching her face. "Everything all right with you, Sadie?"

She took a deep breath, ready to dive in. "Actually, I'm in a bit of a pickle and I'm hoping you can help out."

"Shoot." He stretched out his legs and crossed one ankle over the other, the tips of his alligator-skin cowboy boots pointed toward the dark wooden crossbeams on the ceiling.

"I've learned that someone may be using your auction house to fence stolen goods." She watched his expression closely, looking for some sign of guilt. But all she saw was confusion and shock.

"Fencing stolen goods?" He reached up one hand to scratch his chin. "You sure about that, Sadie?"

"Quite sure." She took a sip of her coffee. "I hate to ask this, Marvin, but did you happen to notice anything strange at the Ferris auction? Anything out of the ordinary? Like a GPS tracker or two?"

He blinked in surprise. "Is this a joke?"

"I'm afraid not. We found a GPS tracker in my friend's mystery box. The stolen item was hidden inside the teddy bear."

He sat up and leaned forward in the chair. "Sadie, are you serious? What are you talking about? What stolen item?"

She took another long sip of coffee to gather her thoughts, not wanting to give him too much information. Her instincts told her that his reaction was genuine, but she didn't know him outside of his professional life. He might be an accomplished liar. "I can't really say."

"Can't or won't?" he asked, his gaze narrowing on her.

"Please understand that I'm not here to accuse you of anything. I thought you should know what's going on. The police are aware that I bought the Steiff teddy bear at the auction. They may be in contact with you, if they haven't been already."

He shook his head. "I haven't heard a peep from the police, but I'll be happy to tell them who's behind this scheme."

That was the last thing she expected to hear. "You know?"

His face darkened. "Leo."

She blinked. "I know you two have parted ways, but do you really think Leo would do something…criminal?"

"I sure wouldn't put it past him. The man's a flannel-mouthed liar," Marvin said bluntly. "He tried to cheat me out of our auction business by using some hotshot lawyer, but it backfired on him and I prevailed. That's probably eating him up inside."

Sadie let his words sink in. "So you really believe Leo could do something like this just for revenge?"

"Revenge. Spite. Call it what you will." A muscle twitched in his cheek. "He's trying to bring me down. I'm just sorry he got you involved, Sadie. If you want, I'll give you the money back for that Steiff bear and deal with the police myself."

His anger was almost palpable, but that didn't mean his accusation against Leo was correct. Marvin could also be trying to deflect attention from himself and on to his former business partner.

"The teddy bear is in the custody of the police, but there is something you can do for me," Sadie said.

"I hope you're going to ask me to string Leo up by his toes, but something tells me it's nothing that satisfying."

She could hear the hurt behind the anger in his words and wondered what it would be like to lose such a good friend in such an ugly way. She couldn't imagine such a rift coming between her and Roz, or any other of her dear friends. Part of her hoped she could prove Marvin wrong, just to leave the possibility open, no matter how small, that he and Leo could mend their friendship someday.

"I'm hoping you can give me some information about the teddy bear's original owner," Sadie replied. "Starla told me on the day of the auction that the owner wished to remain anonymous, but given the circumstances…"

Marvin bolted from his chair. "I'll be right back."

She watched him turn and head down the hallway of the cabin until he was out of sight. As she sipped her coffee, she could hear the *clomp* of his cowboy boots on the wood floor, and a few moments later, he reappeared with a slip of paper in his hands.

"We don't have the name of the seller, but this may help you." Then he handed her the paper.

"A PO box?" she said, setting down her cup and staring at the paper.

He nodded. "That's where we were instructed to send the proceeds from the sale of the teddy bear." He sighed. "It's not our policy to do business without a name and some form of identification, but with Leo out of the picture, things have been a little topsy-turvy around here. Everything was so chaotic the day of the Ferris auction and I didn't want to turn down a Steiff, so I'll admit I cut some corners."

Sadie stood up, not wanting to distress him further. "This helps a lot, Marvin. Thank you."

He gave a brisk nod. "Let me know how it all turns out."

"I will," she promised, and then headed for the door.

Sadie gave the Irish setter another loving pat as she walked out on the porch, then her gaze fell on the paper once more.

PO Box 372
Breckenridge, Colorado 80424

There was no name and no way to identify the owner of the post office box. Which meant Sadie would have to find a way to bring him—or her—out into the open.

11

SADIE STUDIED THE NOTE IN HER HAND, HOPING SHE'D COME UP with the right words to bring the teddy bear's seller out of the woodwork.

She sat in her red Tahoe outside a drugstore in Breckenridge, right across the street from the post office. After purchasing a small stationery set from the store, as well as a postage stamp and a bottle of iced tea, she'd returned to the Tahoe to pen the note.

It had taken her a while to compose, but she'd finally found the right tone.

I know what you did with the Steiff teddy bear. Meet me at the Colorado Mountain College coffee shop on Monday at 2:00 PM. Wear three rubber bands on your left wrist. If you are not there, I will go public with my information.

Since the seller had taken such pains to remain anonymous, Sadie hoped this cryptic note might shake them up enough to meet her on Monday. Or, if they were innocent, to meet her simply out of curiosity. She'd chosen the campus coffee shop because it was always bustling with students and teachers, making it a safer choice than a more secluded spot.

Sadie didn't sign the note, not wanting to give any information about herself. Then she tucked the note into the envelope and sealed it. She added the stamp to the front and then picked up her pen.

She hesitated for a moment, the pen hovering above the envelope before she decided how to address it.

> To Whom It May Concern
> PO Box 372
> Breckenridge, Colorado 80424

There was a good chance that no one would show up at the coffee shop on Monday, but it was a risk she was willing to take. She had to know how that Huntley coin had found its way inside the teddy bear if she wanted to clear herself.

Sadie climbed out of her SUV and walked across the street to the post office. She slipped the envelope into the mail slot on the side of the redbrick building, saying a silent prayer that her plan would work, before returning to the Tahoe.

Then she headed back to Silver Peak. It was almost four o'clock, which meant the school bus would be dropping off Sara at Sadie's house. Sadie hadn't made a dinner plan yet and just didn't feel much like cooking tonight.

Then she got another idea.

She pulled over to the side of the road and then picked up her cell phone and called Edwin.

He answered on the first ring. "Hey, Sadie."

"Hi," she said, smiling at the sound of his voice. "Did I catch you napping?"

He laughed. "I wish, but I'm too busy working this afternoon to enjoy a nap. What's up?"

"I'm on my way back from Breckenridge and I just had a wonderful idea. Why don't we meet up at Sophia's for supper tonight? Sara and I would love the company."

"What time will you two be there?"

"Probably about six, but we're flexible."

"Well, let me see what I can do," Edwin said. "I'll try my best to make it."

Sadie heard something a little odd in his tone she couldn't quite identify. Was it fatigue? Frustration? "Is everything all right, Edwin?"

"Oh yes, Sadie, don't worry. I'm fine. Just a little preoccupied at the moment."

"Well, I won't keep you any longer," she told him, feeling a little better. "Hope to see you later."

"Me too," he said, and then rang off.

Sadie disconnected the call on her phone and then sat staring at it for a few minutes. It just occurred to her that Edwin hadn't called her since getting her out of jail. Had he just been busy or ...

Sadie didn't let herself finish that thought. Instead, she shifted the Tahoe into gear and pulled back onto the highway.

The sunlight filtered through the tree leaves as she drove, and the falling temperature outside made her turn on the heat in the SUV. Other than having a nice chat with Alfred, her trip to Breckenridge had been fairly fruitless. She still didn't know if Marvin was involved in fencing stolen property and she still didn't have the name of the teddy bear's owner.

The clock was ticking down until her court date and Sadie didn't want to walk in there empty-handed. In fact, she didn't want to go at all, hoping to find enough evidence to convince the sheriff to drop the charges against her.

By the time she reached Silver Peak, the sun was setting low in the sky. She drove past the Antique Mine and saw that it was closed up tight for the night. Then she headed home. By the time she got to the house, her stomach was rumbling. She walked inside and was greeted by Hank, who kept sniffing at her ankles.

"You must smell Rufus," she said, leaning down to rub his side. "He's almost as sweet as you."

Footsteps sounded in the hallway and she looked up to see Sara approaching her.

"Hey, Grandma," Sara greeted her. "How was your day?"

"Not bad," Sadie said with a smile. "How about yours?"

Sara frowned. "It was awful, actually. We had a pop quiz in science class and the questions were ridiculously hard. Then we had to play dodge ball in gym class. I hate that game. Lauren hit me right in the face with the ball and it really hurt." She leaned closer and pulled her hair back from her right, freckled cheek. "Is the red mark still there?"

"Nope," Sadie said, leaning closer to give her cheek a kiss. "Still looks perfect and beautiful to me."

"Grandma," Sara exclaimed, rolling her eyes. "You're just saying that to make me feel better."

"I'm saying it because you are perfect and beautiful to me."

"I am not," Sara muttered, although a small smile fluttered on her mouth, revealing the sparkle of her braces for a brief moment.

Sadie set down her purse on the dining room table and then rubbed her chilled hands together. "Well, I know something that may make you feel better. How about supper at Sophia's?"

Sara's hazel eyes flashed with delight. "Really?"

Sadie nodded. "I'm in the mood for pizza and definitely not in the mood for cooking."

"Can I ask Mia to come with us?"

"Sure," Sadie told her granddaughter. "We can pick her up on the way. I invited Edwin to eat with us too, although he's not sure he can make it."

Sara frowned. "How come?"

"He's busy with his mayoral duties, I suppose," Sadie said.

"Too busy to eat?"

Sadie was a little surprised at Sara's reaction, but maybe she didn't want her grandmother to feel like a third wheel. Or, more likely, she wanted to be able to talk to Mia without Grandma listening in.

"I'm going to take Hank for a short hike and then I'll be ready to go. Do you want to come with us?"

Sara shook her head. "No, I need to finish a few math questions and then I want to curl my hair."

"Okay," Sadie said, glancing at her watch. "Let's plan to leave in about forty-five minutes."

"I should be ready by then," Sara replied, and then headed back toward the kitchen. "I'll call Mia and tell her what time we'll pick her up."

Sadie walked into her bedroom and grabbed a dove-gray crewneck sweater out of the closet, pulling it over her powder-blue long-sleeved turtleneck. Then she picked up a pair of gloves and headed toward the front door, where Hank waited for her, his tail wagging behind him.

"Ready, boy?" Sadie asked him, reaching for the doorknob.

He gave an excited bark, and then dashed out the front door. Sadie followed him outside and headed for the trail in the fading twilight.

Sophia's was crowded when Sadie walked through the front entrance, followed by Sara and Mia. Not surprising for a Friday night, Sadie thought to herself, especially when the cozy restaurant only had about a dozen tables. Fortunately, there was one empty table in the far corner of the Tuscan-style restaurant.

The savory aroma of Chef Mark's marinara sauce filled the air, making Sadie's mouth water. His recipe was one of the best-kept secrets in town. Even the *Chatterbox* hadn't discovered the recipe yet, although probably not for lack of trying.

Sadie had worked up an appetite on her hike with Hank, leaving both of them tired and hungry. They'd left Hank at home with a full bowl of dog chow before heading into town.

A young waitress approached them whom Sadie recognized as Beth Deering, Martin and Paula Deering's niece. Beth had joined Martin and Paula for the worship service at Campfire Chapel a time or two. Beth was cute and petite, and her blonde hair was pulled back into a neat ponytail. Her blue-green eyes matched the beaded turquoise necklace she wore with her uniform.

Beth picked up some menus from the table beside her. "Hello there," she greeted them. Then she smiled at Sara. "Back so soon? Where's that cute boy you brought in with you yesterday?"

Sara turned three shades of red. "He's...busy."

Sadie knew Sara had stayed in town after school yesterday to work on a class project, but she'd had no idea Sara had gone to Sophia's with a boy.

"So there's just three tonight?" Beth asked.

"Actually, a fourth may be joining us," Sadie told her, glancing around the restaurant to make certain Edwin wasn't already seated. But he was nowhere in sight. "Edwin Marshall."

Beth's eyes lit in recognition. "Oh, you mean Mayor Marshall?"

"Yes," Sadie replied as Beth led them to their table. She waved to her hairdresser, Sallie Henderson, who was dining with her son, Milo. Then her gaze fell on Ardis and Mable Fleagle, who were dining with their three young children. The young contractor and his wife waved to her and Sadie waved back.

When they reached their table, Sadie and the girls waited a moment while Beth set the menus in place. That's when Sadie's eye caught Kyle Kenmore's gaze on her. The young police officer was out of uniform and sat alone at a small table near the window, a large, half-eaten pizza in front of him.

Kyle quickly looked away from Sadie, pretending he hadn't seen her. His avoidance of her hurt at first, but Sadie tried not to take it personally. After arresting his high school history teacher a few days ago, Kyle probably didn't know how to react to her in public. Perhaps he even thought she was angry with him.

"Excuse me, girls," Sadie told Sara and Mia as they took their seats at the table. "I'll be right back."

She walked over to Kyle's table. "Hello, Kyle."

He looked up at her in surprise and then quickly wiped a spot of pizza sauce off his chin. "Hello, Mrs. Speers."

"I just want you to know there are no hard feelings about what happened at the Antique Mine the other day. I know you were just doing your job."

Relief flashed in his eyes. "Thanks. I'll admit it's been bothering me ever since. I'm probably not supposed to say this, but I'm pretty sure you didn't do it."

She smiled at his careful phrasing. "I appreciate it. And I can promise you that I am innocent of the crime. Now I'm just trying to find a way to prove it."

Concern furrowed his brow. "I hope you're not trying to investigate this case yourself, Mrs. Speers. It's really better handled by professionals like myself."

Sadie bit back another smile. Despite Kyle's years on the police force, she still remembered him as the lanky, awkward teenager in her history class who had described Napoleon as "a really great dessert" in answer to a test question about the Peninsular War. "I'll keep that in mind," she told him, not wanting to worry the boy. "Enjoy your dinner."

"You too," he said with a smile as he reached for another slice of his pepperoni pizza.

Sadie walked back to her table where Mia and Sara were talking with their heads together. They both quieted when Sadie sat down. "So do you girls know what you want to order?"

"We're thinking either the Canadian bacon with pineapple or the veggie pizza."

"They both sound good," Sadie replied, aware that the Canadian bacon and pineapple was one of Edwin's favorites. She glanced up as Beth approached their table. "Let's do an extra-large pizza and make it half veggie and half Canadian bacon with pineapple, along with an order of cheesy bread sticks. That should be plenty of food for the four of us."

"Perfect," Mia said with a smile.

Beth took their pizza order, including drinks, and then headed toward the kitchen to hand it to Mark.

Sadie glanced at her watch as the waitress walked away, noting that it was already a quarter past six. She hoped Edwin would arrive while the pizza was still hot.

A few moments later, Beth brought their drinks, along with three straws. Sadie opened her straw and placed it in the glass of raspberry tea she'd ordered. "So," she said with a smile, looking at Sara, "who is this boy Beth mentioned?"

Sara began to choke on the cola she'd been drinking.

"Are you okay?" Mia asked, reaching over to pat her back.

Sara coughed three times, her cheeks aflame with a deep blush. "Yes, I'm fine," she croaked.

Sadie wasn't sure if the blush was due to embarrassment or the coughing.

"Are you sure, dear?" Sadie asked her. "Have a small bite of the bread stick. Sometimes a little bread can help when you've got something in your throat."

Sara immediately reached into the bread basket and tore off a chunk of the bread stick with her teeth. Then she chewed long and thoughtfully, not quite meeting Sadie's gaze.

Mia reached for a bread stick, too, shortly followed by Sadie. The gooey cheese and herbs mingled in her mouth, along with the warm, fresh bread. If she wasn't careful, Sadie knew she could fill up on bread sticks before their pizza even arrived.

When Sara had fully recovered, Sadie asked her again about the boy. "So what's his name?"

"Tre Havelock," Sara said before quickly taking another bite of her bread stick. "His family just moved to town."

"Are you two an item?" Sadie asked.

Mia giggled, covering her mouth with her hand.

Sara quickly swallowed. "*Grandma!* No! We're just working on a class project together."

Sadie reached for her iced tea. "What class?"

"English," Sara said. "We've got to write a paper together and add photos and graphics and stuff. Tre's really good with computers."

Mia looked at her friend. "But you like him a little, right?"

"Well, he's nice, I guess," Sara said, stumbling over her words a bit. "But we're just friends."

Sadie smiled to herself and then changed the subject. At fourteen, Sara was a little boy-crazy but still too young to start dating.

And speaking of dates, where was Edwin?

Sadie glanced at her watch, noting that it was now six thirty and there was still no sign of him.

About five minutes later, her cell phone buzzed on the table in front of her. She looked down and saw a text from Edwin. As the girls began chatting with each other about school, Sadie opened the text and read it.

Sadie, looks like I'm going to miss out on supper tonight. Wish I could be there. Have fun!

Disappointment washed over her as she placed her cell phone in her purse. He hadn't given her a reason for skipping out, although he'd mentioned earlier that he was busy at work.

Or maybe he'd seen the recent Chatterbox *article and had questioned whether the mayor should be seen in public with a police suspect.*

That thought made Sadie feel a little sick inside, so she brushed it away. Edwin wasn't the type of man to let the opinions of an anonymous blogger dictate his behavior.

He wasn't the type of man who had to bail his girlfriend out of jail either. Sadie nibbled her lower lip, wondering if he might be having second thoughts about their relationship.

Beth's arrival at the table broke that disturbing train of thought.

"Here you go," Beth announced, as she set a pizza platter on the terra-cotta trivet in the center of the table. "One extra-large half veggie and half Canadian bacon with pineapple. Now, may I get you anything else?"

Sadie smiled up at her. "I think we're fine for now."

"Okay, enjoy," Beth said, before heading off to another table.

Sara and Mia each helped themselves to a slice of veggie pizza, then exchanged the glass shakers of parmesan cheese and red pepper flakes to add the finishing touches.

"This looks amazing," Sara said, before picking up the slice in front of her and taking a bite.

Sadie reached for the wedge-shaped spatula and placed a thick slice of Canadian bacon and pineapple pizza on her plate.

Now that Edwin wasn't joining them, she'd have plenty of leftovers.

Or maybe they could stop by his house on the way home and give him some of the pizza to enjoy.

No, she told herself. If Edwin had time to see her tonight, he would have been here. She'd probably see him tomorrow or on Sunday at church. That would give her time to get over this silly notion that he was avoiding her.

By Sunday morning, Sadie hadn't heard another word from Edwin. She'd spent most of Saturday working at the Antique Mine and interacting with her customers.

Sara had arrived in the afternoon to help her and they'd had fun working together. Alice and Theo had called last evening and told them more stories about the college tours. From the sound of it, Theo and Alice were both having a marvelous time on their trip.

Now, on Sunday morning, as she sat in a pew at Campfire Chapel, Sadie glanced around the sanctuary in search of Edwin but didn't see him anywhere.

Sadie had left room for him at the end of the pew and Sara sat on the other side of her, paging through the hymnal, while two-year-old Caleb Henderson, the son of Wyatt and Jenna Henderson, made faces at them from two rows up.

Sadie smiled at Caleb and then blew him a kiss. He giggled at her and then placed his chubby little hand on his mouth and blew a kiss back at her.

A moment later, Paula Deering began playing "Morning Has Broken" on the piano as Pastor Don Sweeting walked slowly to the front of the church, greeting congregation members as he passed, and then finally taking his place behind the pulpit.

Pastor Don lifted his arms in the air as the last notes of the song reverberated in the room. "Morning has broken," he exclaimed with a smile. "Rejoice in the day the Lord has made."

Sadie winked at Caleb and then focused her attention on the pastor. Sunlight streamed through the stained-glass windows of the clapboard church, painting a rainbow of colors over the wood pews. She tried to ignore the empty spot beside her as she listened to the sermon and soon got caught up in the inspiring message.

By the time she stood up to sing the closing hymn, many of Sadie's fears and worries had fallen away, buoyed by her faith and the fellowship of the believers around her.

"I'm starving," Sara whispered after Pastor Don said the benediction.

"You shouldn't have skipped breakfast," Sadie reminded her.

Sara had waited until the last possible moment to hop out of bed this morning and get ready for church, leaving her no time to eat. Sadie had offered the girl a granola bar, but Sara had turned it down.

Paula began playing "Just a Closer Walk with Thee" on the piano as the congregation stood up and began to shuffle out of the pews.

"Flapjacks for brunch?" Sara asked.

Sadie waved to Harry Polmiller and the Hendersons before turning to Sara. "Actually, I thought we might pack a picnic lunch and take the horses out this afternoon."

Sara clapped her hands in delight. "That sounds perfect!"

Sadie smiled, pleased with her reaction. Then she looked up and saw Edwin standing a few feet away. He was talking with Jeanne Sweeting and Lanford Ruxton. A moment later, the three of them started laughing.

Sadie wondered why Edwin hadn't sat with her. She hesitated a moment, not certain whether to approach the group or keep going. But the people behind her kept moving and sidling past her and Sara. Eventually, Sadie found herself funneled toward Pastor Don, with Sara close behind her.

"Good morning, ladies," the pastor greeted them. "How are you?"

"Hungry," Sara murmured.

"We're fine," Sadie said with a smile, reaching out to shake his hand. "I enjoyed your message."

"Thank you." Pastor Don fished a piece of cherry licorice from his pocket and held it out to Sara. "Maybe this will hit the spot."

Sara grinned as she took it from him. "Thanks!"

Then they walked outside into the bright sunlight. It was a perfect day for a ride. They'd only gone a few more steps when Sadie heard Edwin's voice behind her.

"Hold up," Edwin called out.

Sadie turned to see Edwin hurrying toward them. Her heart leapt in her chest and she found herself smiling at him. Edwin looked impeccably handsome in his gray dress shirt, black tie, and black slacks. Most folks wore casual clothes to worship services these days, but Edwin's upbringing in a more formal church showed in his choice of attire.

Sara stood beside her as Edwin approached them, chewing on the piece of licorice that Pastor Don had given her.

"I was afraid you'd be gone by the time I got out of there." Edwin reached up one hand to wipe his brow. "Lanford sure does like to talk."

"I didn't see you earlier," Sadie told him, not wanting to ask outright why he hadn't sat with her.

"I arrived late," he said, a note of apology in his tone, "and sat in the back pew so I wouldn't disrupt the service. Then I ran into Lanford and he wanted to talk about the new committee that he and Jeanne will be serving on…"

"Committee?" Sadie interjected.

Edwin arched a white brow. "Oh, didn't I tell you? The town is thinking about purchasing three vacant run-down Victorian houses to restore. Then we'll rent them for residential or retail use."

Sadie smiled. "I think that's a wonderful idea."

He nodded. "We're just in the beginning stages. The town council appointed Lanford, Jeanne, and a few others to the committee. And we've hired Laura to do some consulting work, since she apparently has experience writing grants for projects like this."

Sadie had seen her cousin at Arbuckle's just a few days ago, but Laura hadn't mentioned anything about a new project. Then again, the woman had been so busy lately that it had probably slipped her mind. "Laura will be perfect for that job. She's an excellent writer."

Edwin nodded and then turned to Sara. "How was the pizza Friday night? I was sorry I missed out."

"It was awesome," Sara said. "We even had leftovers." Then her eyes widened as she looked at Sadie. "Can we take some of the leftover pizza on our picnic?"

Sadie smiled. "Cold pizza?"

"Yeah," Sara said, "I like cold pizza even better than hot pizza."

"Well, then, I guess we can," Sadie said, laughing. She looked up at Edwin. "We're going for a horseback ride and a picnic today, if you'd like to join us."

When Edwin hesitated, Sadie held her breath. If he turned her down again, she'd really start to wonder if there was something bothering him.

After a long moment, Edwin smiled and said, "I'd love to join you. What time?"

She glanced at her watch. "Shall we meet at Milo's ranch in about an hour?"

"I'll see you there," Edwin replied, giving them a salute before heading toward the parking lot.

Sadie watched him walk away, happy that he'd accepted her invitation. Now she could spend this lovely, sunny afternoon with two of her favorite people.

12

———

"This is the life." Edwin leaned back on his elbows, the red-and-white-checkered tablecloth providing a thin barrier between him and the grassy meadow. He'd changed out of his suit and into a pair of blue jeans and an orange-and-blue Denver Broncos sweatshirt. Since he was riding Theo's horse, Bronco, today, it was the perfect outfit.

Sadie smiled as she sat beside him, placing the last paper plate in the wicker picnic basket. "It sure is."

The three horses grazed on the lush grass a short distance away. They'd watered them at a creek shortly before stopping for their picnic. Sara nestled in a cozy spot on a low, thick tree branch a few yards away and chatted on her cell phone with Alice. Sadie had talked to her daughter briefly this morning while Sara was in the shower before church. She'd promised Alice that Sara would give her a call this afternoon.

Sadie turned her face to the warm sun and breathed a deep, contented sigh. Milo had treated them to some of his homemade apple cider before they'd left his ranch on horseback. That delicious cider had satisfied them enough to ride for a couple of hours before finally stopping in this peaceful spot for their picnic.

"I wish we didn't have to go back," Sadie said.

Edwin turned his head to look at her. "That doesn't sound like the Sadie I know."

She smiled. "Don't worry, I'm not planning to hide away in the mountains, as tempting as that might be." She took a deep breath. "I suppose you saw the *Chatterbox* post about my arrest."

He sat up. "Yes, I have. Don't tell me you're letting the gossip bother you?"

"No, not really." She turned to face him. "But I think you should step down as my lawyer. Gossip or not, the *Chatterbox* has a point. The mayor of Silver Peak shouldn't be representing his girlfriend in a criminal case."

His blue eyes met hers. "Sadie, I'm not stepping down."

Sadie closed her eyes for a moment, grateful for his support. But there was more at stake here than just their feelings for each other. "Edwin, we don't know what's going to happen. I can find another lawyer…"

"Not one as good as me," he said bluntly. One corner of his mouth tipped up in a smile. "I realize how conceited that must sound, and I don't mean it to be. But I have extensive criminal trial experience. I know how the system works, Sadie, and how to work out a good plea deal…"

"A plea deal?" she interjected, and then shook her head. "No plea deal for me. That means I'd have to say I'm guilty when I'm not guilty of anything, Edwin, except a fondness for Steiff teddy bears. Which is what got me into this mess."

"I know you're not guilty," he said softly. "But they have evidence against you, and until proof to exonerate you surfaces, they may proceed with criminal charges. I'm not trying to scare you, Sadie, I'm just telling you the truth."

"I know," she said, picking a stray bread crumb off the table-cloth and tossing it in the grass.

He sat up. "In a worst-case scenario, we should be able to plead you down to a lesser charge. Most likely a misdemeanor. Then this mess all goes away."

She trusted Edwin and knew she should listen to him, but the thought of pleading guilty to anything made her feel sick inside. Maybe he wanted this mess to go away even more than she did. Sadie had tried to give him an out by suggesting she get a new attorney, but Edwin had refused—as she'd known he would. Edwin Marshall was nothing if not loyal. He'd stand by her through thick and thin.

Edwin moved closer to Sadie and took her hand. His broad fingers entwined with hers and gave them a gentle squeeze. "I'm in this with you all the way."

His words warmed her heart and she found herself smiling.

"Hey, you two," Sara called out. "No funny business!"

Sadie and Edwin both laughed as they turned to see Sara walking toward them. Sadie released Edwin's hand and then stood up. "Did you have a nice talk with your mom?"

"Yeah," Sara replied, twirling a long strand of grass in her hand, "and Theo too. They wish they were here riding with us."

Edwin rose to his feet. "I hope Theo doesn't mind my riding Bronco."

"No, he's cool with it." Sara tossed the blade of grass aside. "Do we have time to ride to the top of the mountain?"

Sadie glanced at Edwin. "We have plenty of daylight to make it to the top and back, if you have time."

"All the time in the world," Edwin said.

After packing all the picnic supplies into the wicker basket, the three of them walked over to the horses.

Sadie grabbed Scout's loose reins and moved closer to gently stroke the chestnut gelding's velvety nose. She fished a carrot from her pocket, a leftover from the picnic, and fed it to him, then looped the reins up around his neck before placing the picnic basket on the back of the saddle.

Moments later, the three of them were mounted and headed back up the trail to the mountain peak. Snow dotted the landscape ahead of them, and a hawk sailed in the blue sky above. Sara prodded her light bay filly, Daisy, forward until she was ahead of Sadie and Edwin on the trail. Edwin pulled next to Sadie and eased Bronco into a steady pace that matched Scout step for step.

Several moments of silence passed between them as they rode, but it was an easy, comfortable silence that didn't call for words. Sadie breathed in the crisp, fresh air and watched Sara's strawberry-blonde ponytail bounce up and down as Daisy trotted ahead of them.

"You know," Edwin said at last, breaking the silence, "at this moment, I wish we didn't have to go back either."

She looked over at him and smiled. "Tempting, isn't it?"

He nodded. "Maybe I should look into building a cabin up here."

"Away from all the hustle and bustle of Silver Peak?" she said, laughing. "Most folks come to Silver Peak to get away from the hustle and bustle of the city."

"I know. And Silver Peak will always be my home. But there's something about being up here—with you—that just feels right."

Sadie's throat tightened at his words. After her fears that he'd been avoiding her—or worse, been embarrassed by her—his sentiment almost made her cry. She swallowed hard, pushing back the emotion before it overwhelmed her. "It feels right to me too. Of course, we haven't raced yet."

He turned to look at her and Sadie gave him a daring grin.

"First one to that big pine tree wins?" she challenged.

He arched a silver brow. "Wins what?"

Sadie thought for a moment, and then said, "How about the last slice of chocolate cake in the picnic basket?"

"Deal."

"On the count of three," Sadie said, leaning forward in the saddle, her hands gripping the reins just a little more tightly. "One."

"Two," Edwin said, his gaze on the tree ahead.

"Three," they said together, and then each spurred their horses into action.

Sadie and Edwin raced past Sara on her horse. Sara hooted behind them. "Go, Grandma!"

Sadie loved the feel of the wind in her hair and the powerful horse beneath her. A competitor at heart, Sadie gave her all to the race. But she knew that no matter which one of them reached the tree first, as long as Edwin was beside her, she'd win.

On Monday morning, Sadie opened her shop and waited for Julie to arrive. She'd awakened early and taken Hank for a long walk after enjoying her morning devotional. But she'd been too nervous about the two o'clock meeting at the Colorado Mountain College campus coffee shop today to eat breakfast.

Now Sadie paced back and forth across the wide plank floor in the Antique Mine, her mind racing. Even though she'd told herself not to get her hopes up, she couldn't help but imagine the upcoming meeting with the mysterious owner of the teddy bear.

Would it be a man or a woman? Young? Old? Somewhere in the middle? And most important of all, would the owner know that a Huntley coin had been hidden inside the teddy bear?

She just hoped the note she'd sent to that post office box was enough to bring the teddy bear's owner out of hiding. She stopped to take a drink of the coffee she'd purchased at Arbuckle's earlier. Luz had tried to tempt her with one of her fresh, home-baked pastries, but the nervous knots in Sadie's stomach didn't leave room for more than her coffee. She hoped she'd be hungry enough to grab a sandwich in Breckenridge before the meeting.

Julie walked through the front door, setting off the bell.

Sadie set down her cup and greeted her with a smile. "Good morning."

"Good morning to you." Julie walked to the front counter and set her purse on the marble countertop. Then she breathed a happy sigh. "I thought I'd never get out of the house this morning. Logan couldn't find his shoes and Brody couldn't find his math book." She shook her head. "And if that wasn't chaotic enough, my husband suddenly remembered that he needed to bring something for the potluck lunch at the clinic today."

Sadie chuckled. "That sounds like a full day's work in itself. I'm surprised you made it here at all."

Julie tucked a lock of blonde hair behind her ear. "I guess I'm used to it. Logan's shoes were in the dog bed. The math book was under Brody's bed. And I sent Chad to work with two bags of corn chips and a jar of salsa."

"All that hustle and bustle and it's not even nine o'clock yet." Sadie smiled. "Now I wish I hadn't asked you to work at the shop this week."

"Are you kidding?" Julie said with a bemused smile. "Working at the Antique Mine seems like a nice vacation compared to herding my two boys." Her smile widened. "Or maybe I should say three boys, even though one is over six feet tall."

Sadie laughed. "Well, vacation or not, I really appreciate everything you do for me."

Sadie walked around the counter and pulled open a drawer. "And I got you a little something." She retrieved a plastic gift card from inside and handed it to Julie.

Julie's eyes widened. "Oh, Sadie! Thirty dollars at Arbuckle's? You shouldn't have!"

"After the way your day started, you deserve it."

Julie smiled as she walked over and gave Sadie a hug. "How about if I buy us breakfast? Maybe two cinnamon rolls to go?"

"Thanks, but I'll pass," Sadie told her. She reached for her purse. "I do need to go though. Give me a call if you have any problems."

"I'll be fine," Julie said. "Have a fun day."

"Thanks, I'll try." Sadie slipped her purse over her shoulder and walked out of the Antique Mine. She wasn't sure how fun her day might be, but she definitely had a full schedule.

Her first stop was at the American Mining Company, located in a grand, brick Victorian that had once served as a schoolhouse in Silver Peak.

A yellow school bus sat outside the museum, along with a few other cars. She parked in an empty space and then made her way into the museum.

A group of elementary-school children were milling about the main foyer, looking at some of the artwork from the Silver Rush era and exclaiming over several of the large minerals on display in glass cases. Sadie waited until their teacher led them into the Copper Room before making her way to the reception desk, where the museum curator, Clive Selby, stood flipping through some papers in a folder.

Clive looked up as she approached. "Hello, Sadie. May I help you?"

"I hope so," she said. "I'm wondering if you can tell me the name of the silversmith who used this maker's mark." She showed him the picture of the archer's bow engraved on the back of Harry's platter.

His eyes popped. "I sure can. That's Eustace Huntley's mark."

"Huntley?" Sadie's heart skipped a beat. "He wouldn't by any chance be the man who minted the Huntley silver dollars? The exact replicas of the Morgan silver dollars?"

Clive looked impressed. "One and the same. How did you know?"

As soon as he asked the question, Sadie saw the wheels turning in Clive's brain. He'd obviously read about her arrest for possessing one of the Huntley counterfeit coins. She had to press her mouth together to keep from proclaiming her innocence.

Clive cleared his throat. "We don't have much information about Eustace Huntley, I'm sorry to say." He motioned for Sadie to follow him and led her to the History Room. It was filled with old sepia photographs of miners and the boomtown period of Silver Peak, along with several books and framed maps.

Clive pointed out a small display case. "We have a few silver items that were forged by Eustace before his arrest, but none of the ten counterfeit coins that eventually got him into so much trouble."

Clive scooted over, making room for Sadie to have a closer look.

"As you can see," he continued, "the man was quite talented. It really was a shame that he used that talent for such a nefarious purpose."

Sadie stared at the silver pieces designed and forged by Eustace Huntley. There was an intricate cup, a large silver medallion engraved with a finely detailed outline of the Rocky Mountains, and a small silver baby rattle. The workmanship was excellent—just like the Huntley coin that had fallen out of the teddy bear.

A telephone began to ring in the next room. "Excuse me," Clive said. "I need to answer that."

"Go right ahead," Sadie told him. "I'll be fine here on my own."

Clive left the room, leaving Sadie alone. She saw a small framed newspaper article from 1905 next to the medallion and leaned closer to read it.

Eustace Huntley had been sentenced to twelve years' hard labor at the Colorado State Penitentiary for passing counterfeit Morgan silver dollars resulting in theft of goods. According to the judge presiding over the trial, the stiff prison sentence was to serve as a warning to others who might use their talents to break the law. Huntley was known as one of the best silversmiths in the state of Colorado before his arrest.

Clive was right, it was a shame. She wondered how Harry would feel about the fact that his beloved grandmother's silver platter had been forged by a criminal.

Should she even tell him?

It was a question that niggled at her as she drove out of Silver Peak and made her way to Breckenridge.

Leo Best sat at a wobbly desk in his small office in Breckenridge. He was a thin man, close to sixty, with angled cheekbones that jutted from his sallow face. A few long strands of gray hair were combed over the top of his bald head, making him look like a much older man.

Sadie had tracked him down through the Internet last evening and discovered that he'd opened his own business, Best Auction Services, just a few weeks ago.

Unlike his old partner, Marvin, Leo had his office in the heart of downtown Breckenridge, smack in the center of a run-down strip mall.

Since she had some time before her two o'clock meeting at the campus coffee shop, Sadie had decided to check in with Leo and see if he could offer any information about Marvin and the possible fencing of stolen goods.

Leo stood up as she walked through the door. "Sadie Speers! My, but you're a sight for sore eyes."

Sadie smiled. "How are you, Leo?"

"I'm good," he said, motioning her toward a chair. "Better than I've been in a while. How about you?"

"I'm well," she said, taking a seat. "How do you like your new office?"

"Not bad," he said with a nod. "I assume you've heard that I decided to go solo."

"Yes, I found out at the Ferris estate auction."

"Marv and I were supposed to work that auction together, but somehow he ended up with it."

Sadie heard the bitterness in his voice and once more felt sadness at the broken friendship. "Marvin told me that you two were having problems."

Leo nodded. "I've suspected him of cheating me out of some of the profits for quite some time. In fact, I even hired a forensic accountant a few months ago to investigate the matter."

"And?" Sadie asked.

"And nothing," Leo muttered. "Any financial discrepancies the accountant found he determined to be immaterial."

"So no fraud?"

"None." Leo raked one hand over his bald head, dislodging the few gray hairs so carefully placed there. "I don't know what to make of it, Sadie. My wife thinks I jumped the gun by accusing Marvin of trying to swindle me."

"Maybe you two can still work it out?"

Leo shook his head. "That ship has sailed. Besides, I'm better off on my own." He cleared his throat. "In addition to my auction services, I'm also offering appraisal services, so feel free to send any interested parties my way." He plucked a handful of business cards from his desk and handed them to her. "I'm even giving a discount to the first five customers."

"Thanks," Sadie said, rising to her feet and taking the cards from him. "I'll make these available in my shop."

He smiled. "I'd appreciate it. Now, is there anything else I can do for you?"

She shook her head. "No, thank you. I just wanted to ask you about Marvin. There had been some question about the possible fencing of stolen goods through his auctions, but it sounds like your accountant would have caught it."

Leo released a deep sigh. "Yes, he definitely would have caught something like that. Part of me is glad it's not true. But…" His words trailed off. "I guess it's all water under the bridge now."

She chatted with him for a few more minutes, reminiscing about past estate auctions he'd run and some of the unusual items in them.

By the time she left Leo's office, Sadie found just enough time to grab a quick sandwich at the Drover Dell Diner before making her way to the campus coffee shop.

She'd asked the teddy bear's owner to wear three rubber bands around his or her left wrist, but she had no idea if that request would be met. As Sadie walked inside, she looked slowly around, wondering if anyone would meet her at all.

She scanned the patrons, most of them young college students sipping coffee, their laptop computers open in front of them. The coffee shop gave off a sixties-era vibe, with music from the Monkees playing over the stereo speakers and beaded strings hanging in the open doorway between the coffee shop and the bookstore next door.

Sadie checked her watch. It was ten minutes before two o'clock. She walked over to the counter and ordered a cup of coffee. Then she made her way to an empty table. As she walked, she wondered if the seller had spotted her.

She sat down at the table, slipping the strap of her purse over the back of her chair.

Then she waited.

Ever since she'd left Leo's office, Sadie had been thinking about the rift that had developed between Marv and Leo. A rift that had grown from misunderstandings and distrust. A rift that had destroyed a decades-old friendship and a prosperous business partnership. She prayed that the two men would find their way back to each other. And that time would heal the deep wounds between them.

"Oh my gosh, it's you!"

Sadie looked up to see Valerie, Alfred's graduate assistant, staring at her.

"Hello, Val. How are you?" Then Sadie's gaze fell to the three red rubber bands on Val's left wrist. Her heart skipped a beat as she looked up at the girl's pale face. "You?"

Val sank into the empty chair opposite Sadie. "I don't know what to say. I was so scared when I got your letter. Please don't tell Professor Daly what I did!"

Sadie stared at Val, her mind spinning. Guilt was written all over the girl's face. Had she actually placed the Huntley coin inside the teddy bear? If so, that meant Val had probably stolen it as well.

The silence between them grew as Sadie tried to sort out her thoughts. Despite only meeting Val one time, she never would have expected her to be involved in criminal activities.

"How did this happen?" Sadie asked at last.

Val shook her head. "I don't know. It was a stupid thing to do. Mom always said I was too impulsive for my own good. I didn't think anyone would find out."

"Oh, Val," Sadie breathed, truly hoping the girl hadn't been involved in the theft at Brent Fielder's house. "Someone did find out. The police have gotten involved."

Horror filled Val's eyes. "The police!"

Her outcry caused several other patrons to turn and look toward their table. Sadie leaned forward and lowered her voice so only Val could hear her. "Possessing stolen property is a crime," Sadie told her.

Val blinked. "But I only had the teddy bear for the weekend."

"The weekend?" Sadie stared at her, confused. "You're the one who put it up for sale at the Ferris auction, right?"

"Yes, at the request of the owner."

"You mean the Steiff bear didn't belong to you?"

Val shook her head. "No, it belonged to Professor Daly."

13

A COLD CHILL SWEPT THROUGH SADIE. "THERE MUST BE SOME mistake."

"Wait," Val said, holding up one hand. "I thought that note meant you knew what I did. I was afraid you were going to tell Professor Daly."

Three students sat down at an empty table close to Sadie and Val. Sadie didn't want anyone to overhear their conversation, especially now that Alfred was involved. "Is there somewhere else we can talk? Somewhere more private?"

Val nodded as she rose to her feet. "My dorm room. It's pretty close." ·

Sadie left her coffee behind as she and Val walked out of the campus coffee shop and headed toward Val's dorm. Neither one of them spoke, the air thick between them. Sadie couldn't believe that the Steiff teddy bear really belonged to Alfred. He would have said something when Sadie told him she bought a Steiff at the Ferris auction—especially after she showed him the picture of it.

No, Val had to be lying. It would be one way to deflect blame from herself. And why had she acted so guilty when she'd first sat down at the table? Except...she had seemed really sincere.

Soon, they were at the dorm and Val was leading the way down the hall. Val stopped in front of room 105 and placed her key card in the slot. After a *click*, she turned the knob and opened the door, letting Sadie enter first.

A young woman sat at one of the two desks in the room, her black hair swept up into a loose bun. A young man with the same black hair sat on the edge of the desk, swinging one long leg, his glasses sitting halfway down his nose.

"Oh, hi," Val said, greeting the pair. "I thought you had a class, May."

"It got canceled." May swiveled in her chair to face them. "But I have to take Alex to the auto shop to pick up his car."

Val blushed a little as she looked at the young man. "Car trouble?"

He smiled. "Nothing major. Just needed an oil change."

"That's good," Val said, and then cleared her throat as she motioned to Sadie. "This is Mrs. Speers. She's a friend of Professor Daly's." Then Val pointed to the pair at the desk. "This is my roommate, May Cooley, and her brother, Alex."

"We're twins," Alex said with a grin, and then pointed to his sister. "She's the bad one."

"Alex," May chastised, batting him with her pencil. "Behave."

"It's nice to meet you," Sadie told them. "Don't let us chase you out."

"Oh, you're fine," May said, rising to her feet. "I need to go work at the studio after I drop Alex off."

Val turned to Sadie. "May is a fashion design major. She spends most of her time at the design studio."

Alex walked over to the door, pausing long enough to shake Sadie's hand. "Nice to meet you, Mrs. Speers."

"Nice to meet you too, Alex."

May grabbed a couple of textbooks and followed her brother out the door. "Later, Val."

"'Bye," Val called after them. Then she closed the door and turned to Sadie. "Sorry about that. I thought May would be in class."

"That's all right," Sadie told her, moving farther into the small room. A bunk bed and a dressmaker's dummy filled one side of the room while the two desks stood against another wall. A large, bright orange shag rug covered most of the linoleum floor and matched the orange chevron and white coverlet on the bottom bunk bed.

"You can sit in May's chair," Val said, pulling out a chair from the other desk and taking a seat. Then she met Sadie's gaze. "Are you going to tell Professor Daly what I did?"

Sadie walked over to the chair and sat down. "First, why don't you tell me exactly what you did do."

"But you already know."

Sadie didn't want to reveal too much, not sure whether she could trust the girl. Instead, she decided to ask some leading questions and see where they went. "When did Professor Daly give you the teddy bear?"

"Well, he didn't give it to me, exactly," Val said. "He'd arranged to sell it at the Ferris auction and asked me to deliver it there. I already had a post office box that I use for my address on my Facebook page. That way no goofballs can track me down to my dorm room."

"I see," Sadie said. "So Professor Daly asked to use it?"

Val shook her head. "No, I offered. I knew he wanted to keep the sale of the teddy bear a secret." She gave a slight shrug of her shoulders. "I wasn't sure why, but he seemed pretty adamant about it. I wasn't even supposed to say anything to his wife if she called the office."

"Cecile," Sadie breathed, shocked at Val's words. As far as she knew, Alfred and Cecile had never kept secrets from each other. Why now? And why about something as seemingly innocent as selling a Steiff teddy bear?

Unless it wasn't so innocent.

The very thought that Alfred could be involved with putting the coin in the teddy bear made Sadie's mind reel. Yet she couldn't help but wonder why he hadn't told her the teddy bear she'd bought at the auction had belonged to him.

"So anyway," Val continued, "I delivered the teddy bear to the auctioneer and gave them my post office box number to send the money."

"But you did more than that," Sadie said, letting the words linger.

Val groaned. "I wish I could go back and change it. I'd just never seen a teddy bear worth that much money before. And I thought it would be safer with me than sitting in the professor's office all weekend."

"So you brought it here," Sadie surmised, now better understanding the girl's guilty conscience, "without Alfred's permission?"

Val looked down at her hands, twisting her fingers together. "He left early on Friday afternoon while I was still working on some papers in his office. The bear was so cute and I didn't think it would do any harm to bring it back to my dorm room. I kept it in the plastic bag the whole time. And then, first thing on Monday morning, I took it to the auction site."

"Did you put anything in the bear?" Sadie asked her.

Val blanched. "What?"

Her reaction seemed genuine, but Sadie had to be sure. "There was something found inside the teddy bear—something valuable. Did you know about that?"

"No, the professor didn't say anything about it." She looked at Sadie, her eyes wide. "Why would he hide something inside the bear?"

"I don't know that he did," Sadie said quickly. But deep inside, she was having trouble thinking of any other explanation. "Was there anyone else who had access to the bear?" Sadie asked her. "Did you show it to anyone?"

"A few people," Val said, wincing. "I didn't say where I got it though. Everybody thought it was cute."

Sadie nibbled her lower lip, wanting to cover all the bases. "And you never let it leave your dorm room?"

"Never," Val said resolutely. "It went straight from the professor's office on Friday afternoon, to this room for the weekend, and to the auction on Monday morning."

Sadie took a moment to let it all sink in. She knew there was a chance that Val wasn't telling her the entire truth, but just the fact that the Steiff bear had belonged to Alfred changed everything.

He'd lied to Sadie. And he'd asked Val to keep a secret from Cecile. Just those two facts alone made her feel sick inside.

"Is there anything else you can tell me?" Sadie asked her.

Val looked thoughtful for a moment and then shook her head. "No, nothing." Then her gaze narrowed on Sadie. "Are you going to tell Professor Daly what I did?"

Sadie hesitated. "I don't think so. Not yet, anyway." She took a deep breath. "Honestly, Val, it would be better if you just told him yourself. The Alfred I know…" *Or thought I knew.* Sadie cleared her throat. "He wouldn't hold something like that against you. Either way, I believe you'll feel better if you're honest with him."

"I know you're right," Val muttered. "I just need to work up the nerve to do it."

Sadie stood up, ready to take her leave so she could start processing everything Val had told her. "Will you do me one favor?"

"If I can," Val replied.

"Don't tell Professor Daly about our conversation. I'd rather do that myself."

Val nodded. "Okay."

Sadie walked toward the door. That was when she noticed a calendar hanging on the wall beside the closet. Several of the days had been marked with a bright purple pen. But one day in particular stood out to her.

"Is this your calendar?" Sadie asked, turning to look at Val.

Val moved closer to her. "Yes, why?"

"You have *Brent Fielder* written down on the second day of this month. Do you know him?"

"Not really," Val replied. "He had a seminar at his house about Colorado history. I thought it might be interesting to go just to see his famous collections, but the guy turned out to be a pompous jerk. He even made fun of me when I asked him a simple question."

"What was the question?" Sadie asked, curious.

"Well, when the seminar first started, Mr. Fielder asked everyone to state their name and occupation." A muscle flexed in Val's jaw. "When it was my turn, I said I was pursuing my master's degree in history. Later in the day, I asked Mr. Fielder if he'd ever considered lending some of his artifacts to museums." She sniffed. "And he said it wasn't up to him to create more jobs for history majors by cluttering up museums with private collections."

Sadie could hear the emotion in her voice. The man had embarrassed her in front of other people. But would that be enough for Val to seek revenge by stealing some of his collections?

"What did you do?" Sadie asked her.

"Nothing," Val said softly. "I just stopped asking questions and waited for the seminar to end so I could leave." Anger flashed in her eyes. "And I hope I never see Brent Fielder again. In fact…" Her words trailed off as Val grabbed a pen from her desk and then walked over to the calendar. She scribbled the pen across Brent Fielder's name until it was no longer visible. "There," Val said with a satisfied smile, "that's better."

Sadie watched her expression. "And only a few days after that seminar, someone broke into Fielder's house and stole those ten Huntley counterfeit coins, along with a few other things."

"Yeah," she said, a smile threatening at the corner of her lips. "Too bad for him."

Sadie wasn't sure how to interpret that smile. Maybe Val had sought revenge against Fielder by taking some of his property. Or perhaps she just believed that Fielder deserved his fate. Either way, Val didn't look guilty. Certainly not as guilty as she'd appeared in the coffee shop when she'd realized Sadie had sent that note.

"I'll let you get back to your studies," Sadie said, opening the door.

"Okay." Val followed her into the hallway. "And I'll find a way to tell Professor Daly the truth. But it might take me a few days."

Sadie nodded, and then waved good-bye. It might take her a few days to approach Alfred too. How would she ask her friend why he'd lied to her—even if it was a lie of omission?

Something told Sadie she'd be trying to answer that question all the way back to Silver Peak.

Hank bounded toward Sadie as she walked into her house later that afternoon. She leaned down to give him a hug and vigorously rubbed the fur on his back. "You're just the medicine I need," she said with a smile.

Hank's tail wagged as he looked up at her.

Sadie slipped off her fleece jacket and set her purse on the table. That's when she heard her cell phone buzz. She pulled it out of her purse and saw a text from Sara.

Working late at school. Elena will bring me home around six. Is that okay?

Elena Garza was Mia's older sister and a very responsible girl. Sadie tapped in the letters on the phone's keyboard to reply to the text. *Yes, that's fine. See you then.*

She'd put together a tuna casserole last night, so she pulled it out of the refrigerator and turned on the oven to preheat it. Then she turned to Hank, who had followed her into the kitchen.

"How about a walk?" she said, causing the dog to jump once in the air and bark.

Sadie laughed as she made her way to her room. She changed her shoes and grabbed a heavier jacket from her closet, then headed back toward the kitchen to place the tuna casserole in the oven.

She let Hank outside first and then headed out into the yard. The sun sat high in the sky, and puffy white clouds slowly cruised overhead.

Hank led the way on the trail, weaving in and out of trees and chasing rabbits through the bushes. That was one of his favorite games, although he never caught one. Every once in a while, Hank would stop on the trail and look back at Sadie, waiting for her to catch up with him.

After walking about half a mile, Sadie stopped to rest on a flat boulder. Hank trotted over and sniffed her hands before running off into the brush.

Sadie could hear the peaceful gurgle of a stream nearby and leaned down to pick a tiny wildflower peeking through the rocky terrain. She twirled it between her fingers for a moment, her thoughts turning once more to Alfred.

"Oh, Lord, what should I do?" she prayed out loud.

At this point, there were two people most likely to have placed the Huntley coin in the teddy bear. One was Alfred and the other was Val. On the one hand, Val had been in Brent Fielder's house shortly before the theft and could have figured out a way in without detection.

On the other hand, Alfred hadn't told Sadie she'd purchased his Steiff teddy bear. She wondered if he would have said anything if she'd told him the Huntley coin was found inside and she had been arrested because of it.

Sadie wanted to believe he would have told her immediately, but she really couldn't say for sure. She slipped her hand into her jacket and curled her hand around her cell phone. Ever since she'd left the college campus, Sadie had been on the verge of calling Alfred. But even now, she couldn't quite do it. She needed to know more before she approached him.

She needed to know that he was innocent of the crime.

The image of Leo and Marvin flashed in her mind. Their longtime friendship had been ruined by misunderstandings and growing distrust. She'd never forgive herself if she did or said anything to Alfred to cause such a rift in their friendship.

Reaching into her other pocket, Sadie pulled out a water bottle and took a long sip. Someone had framed her after she'd bought that teddy bear, and it just wasn't possible that Alfred had knowingly done so.

She couldn't be so sure about Val, having just met the woman, but her instincts told her that Val wouldn't have the stomach for that kind of treachery.

As she closed the cap on the water bottle, Sadie realized that she needed to talk to Brent Fielder. Perhaps he had some ideas about who might have committed the theft.

Hank bounded out of the bushes and headed straight for Sadie. His paws and legs were wet, along with the underside of his belly.

"Looks like you've been playing in the creek again," she said with a smile. She rose to her feet and started down the trail. "C'mon, buddy. Time to go home."

As they walked toward the house, Sadie tried to let go of the jumble of thoughts that had been whirling around in her head. She wanted to have a nice evening with Sara since the girl would only be staying a few more days.

As she reached the path leading to the back of the house, Sadie noticed a blue pickup truck driving toward the house. Elena drove a small Honda, so she knew it couldn't be Sara.

But as Sadie reached the back gate, she saw the pickup truck turn into her driveway. A teenage boy she didn't recognize sat behind the wheel. And Sara was sitting beside him in the passenger seat.

Sadie walked through the back door, wondering what had happened to the original plan. The savory aroma of tuna casserole filled the room, making her mouth water. Hank headed straight for his dog dish and began munching on the nuggets there.

After shedding her jacket, Sadie walked over to the oven and pulled on a pair of oven mitts. Then she opened the oven door and took out the casserole, placing the hot glass dish on top of the stove.

Sara walked through the kitchen door as Sadie tugged off the oven mitts.

"Hey, Grandma. Something smells delicious."

"Tuna casserole," Sadie said, as Hank turned away from his food bowl and padded over to Sara. "How was your day?"

"Great."

"Why did you have to stay after school?"

Sara turned toward the cupboard, opening it to retrieve a glass. "Oh, Mia wanted me to stay with her while she finished up an art project. Elena was staying late too, so she gave me a ride home."

Sadie stared at her. "That was nice of her. Doesn't Elena have to work at her parents' restaurant this evening?"

"I guess not." Sara moved to the sink and filled up the glass.

Sadie couldn't believe Sara was lying to her. Was it something in the air? First, Alfred and now her sweet granddaughter. "Maybe I'll call Elena and thank her myself." She reached for her cell phone.

Sara whirled around. "No, Grandma, that's not necessary. I already thanked her."

Sadie stared at her for a long moment. Then she said softly, "Sara, I saw that boy drop you off."

Sara's cheeks turned red. "You...did?"

"Yes," Sadie said, remaining calm. She was more hurt than angry. "Why did you lie to me about it?"

Sara sucked in a deep breath. "I thought you'd be mad if you knew I rode in a car with a boy. Elena was supposed to bring me home, but she got called in to work by her mom. That's when Tre said he'd bring me here."

The girl's explanation revealed another lie. "This is the boy who's working on the English project with you?"

Sara nodded, her face still flushed. "That's right."

"Well, if Tre is old enough to drive, that means he's at least sixteen. I don't know many sixteen-year-olds who take freshman English."

Sara visibly gulped. "Um..."

Sadie held up one hand. "Before you say anything more," she said quietly, "please make sure it's the truth."

Hank padded between them looking back and forth, as if sensing the tension in the air.

"Okay," Sara said, her gaze locked on the floor and her voice almost a whisper. "The truth is that Tre is seventeen and a junior. When Elena couldn't drive me here, he offered me a ride and I thought it would be okay."

"If you thought it would be okay, why did you lie to me?"

Tears swam in Sara's eyes. "I guess I didn't want you to find out and be mad."

Sadie walked over to give her a hug. "I'm not angry. I just want you to know that you can always be honest with me." She smoothed one hand over Sara's strawberry-blonde hair. "Okay?"

Sara sniffed. "Okay."

Sadie gave her an extra squeeze for good measure. "And no more rides with Tre or any other boy when you're under my care. I don't want to get in trouble with your mom. Next time, call me, and I'll come pick you up."

Sara gave her a tremulous smile and shook her head. "No more rides."

"Good." Sadie rounded the table and saw Hank wagging his tail as he trotted back to his dog dish. "Now, let's eat."

Later that evening, Sadie sat in the living room with her laptop open beside her. A small fire burned in the hearth, providing the only light in the room other than the glow of her computer screen. Hank had gone upstairs with Sara an hour ago and both of them were probably sleeping by now.

They'd enjoyed an evening of popcorn while watching *The Maltese Falcon* after supper, the earlier tension about Sara's lie completely gone.

But Alfred's deception still weighed heavily on Sadie. She'd been wavering back and forth about calling him, not certain what to say. She knew they'd have to talk sometime—and soon.

Her mind drifted to her trip to the American Mining Museum this morning and the information she'd learned about Eustace

Huntley. Picking up her computer and setting it on her lap, Sadie logged in to Ancestry.com, wondering if Eustace had any descendants still living in the area.

She put the name *Eustace Huntley* in the search engine and waited for the results to load on the page. Soon, names and dates filled the screen. She saw the names of Eustace's parents and siblings, but, according the Web site, Eustace had no direct descendants and had never married.

Sadie closed the laptop with a sigh and set it aside. Her mind drifted back to Alfred, and she realized that she couldn't go on suspecting the worst of him. Not after they'd been such good friends for so many years.

Picking up her cell phone, she dialed a number that she knew by heart. As soon as the other line picked up, Sadie said, "We need to talk."

14

THE NEXT MORNING, SADIE TOOK A DEEP BREATH AND KNOCKED on the front door of the two-story brick bungalow. The door opened and Alfred stood on the other side.

"Hello, Sadie," he said, looking more solemn than she'd ever seen him. "Please, come in."

Sadie walked inside the smart living room. A white leather sofa and matching love seat were arranged in front of the black marble fireplace. A colorful Tiffany-style folding glass fire screen adorned the front of the hearth. Sadie had been in the Dalys' house countless times before, but she almost felt like a stranger as she followed Alfred through the living room and into the kitchen.

Cecile's tasteful decorative flair was evident all through the house, but Sadie could see Alfred's influence in the scrolled woodwork in the hallway and the Albert Bierstadt picture that hung above the fireplace. The Bierstadt print had been an anniversary gift for Cecile. Famous for paintings of the westward expansion and Colorado landscapes in the late nineteenth century, Bierstadt even had a lake named after him in the Rocky Mountain National Park.

"Coffee?" Alfred offered, walking over to the coffeepot by the stove.

"Yes, thank you." Sadie took a seat at the table, wondering if he'd told Cecile about the meeting before she'd left for work this morning. Sadie hadn't said much to Alfred during their phone call last night, wanting to have this conversation in person.

Surprisingly, he hadn't really questioned Sadie about the lateness of her call or her insistence to meet as soon as possible. Something told her that he knew what she was going to say.

A moment later, he set a steaming coffee mug in front of Sadie and then sat down in a chair on the opposite side of the table. He cupped his own coffee mug in his hands and then met her gaze. "You know about the teddy bear, don't you?"

Sadie nodded. Her instincts had been right.

He breathed a long sigh. "Oh, Sadie, I don't even know where to start. What you must think of me…"

Sadie leaned forward. "I think you've been my friend for over thirty years and that you must have had a good reason for not telling me the Steiff bear I bought at the auction belonged to you."

"A reason, yes," he said. "But I'm not sure how good it is."

She studied his face, seeing more worry lines around his eyes and mouth than she'd noticed before. Then her gaze fell to the brown, silk bow tie he wore with his white dress shirt. Surprisingly, the bow tie looked a little frayed at the corners—something she'd never noticed before. Then Sadie remembered the lunch box on his desk the day she'd come to his office to ask his opinion about the coin. Suddenly, all the pieces seemed to come together.

"I know it's none of my business," Sadie began gently. "But are you having financial difficulties?"

A wry smile tipped up one corner of his mouth. "Is it that obvious?"

"No," she said. "It didn't occur to me until just now. But I simply can't think of any other reason you'd sell your Steiff bear. I know how much it meant to you."

He gave a slight nod, his gaze on his coffee mug. "Yes, I'm in something of a pickle, Sadie. And it's all my own doing, I'm afraid."

Sadie took a sip of her coffee, not wanting to push him. She knew he'd tell her in his own good time.

"It began about three months ago," he said. "I made an investment in a sure thing." He shook his head. "I must be getting dotty in my old age, to believe a sure thing even exists. The worst of it is that I used some of the retirement money that Cecile and I have been saving for years." His voice tightened. "And the next thing I knew, it was all gone."

Sadie winced, imagining the horror that Alfred must have felt. And the guilt.

"Does Cecile know?"

"No," he said hoarsely, "not about the lost money or the sale of my Steiff." He finally looked up at Sadie. "I had big plans to surprise her with the hefty dividends from the investment. It never occurred to me that I'd lose it all." He took a long sip of his coffee, the cuckoo clock ticking in the silence between them. "Since then, I've been trying to repay the funds I took out of our retirement savings. Selling some of my personal treasures, including the Steiff teddy bear, is just part of my penance. I just wish it was enough to cover what I lost."

Sadie leaned forward, wanting to offer help. She had a little money squirreled away for a rainy day. But before she could say anything, Alfred held up one hand. "No, Sadie, I've got to do this on my own. It's my folly. I'm the one who needs to pay for it."

"Oh, Alfred," she said, well aware that he could be as stubborn as a mule when the mood struck him. Cecile sometimes even jokingly called him Francis, referring to the talking mule from the movies in the 1950s.

"Sadie, I owe you an apology," he said. "You caught me off guard the day you came into my office with the picture of my Steiff bear, telling me you'd purchased it at the auction. I was ashamed of my money problems and didn't know how to tell you why I'd sold the bear. So I took the coward's way out and just kept my mouth shut."

"I understand," she said. "I admit that it rattled me when I learned the teddy bear belonged to you. I just couldn't imagine why you hadn't told me." She shook her head. "That's why I wanted to come to you and ask."

"And I'm sorry for not telling you sooner." Alfred got up from his chair and retrieved the coffeepot from the counter, topping off both of their mugs. "But you haven't told me yet how you figured it out. Not that I'm surprised you did."

Sadie realized that he still didn't know about her own troubles. Alfred hadn't been the only one keeping secrets. "I had a reason to search for the owner of the teddy bear. Marv Burton told me the owner wanted to remain anonymous, but he did give me the post office box number where the proceeds of the sale were to be sent. So I wrote a letter, wording it in such a way to, I hoped, ferret out the seller. Then I mailed it to the post office box."

He arched a white brow. "Ah, I see. That must have been some letter. Now I understand why Val came to me yesterday and confessed that she'd taken the Steiff to her dorm room the weekend before the estate auction. She didn't mention your letter though."

Now it was Sadie's turn to squirm a little. "We had agreed to not mention our meeting to you."

Alfred nodded. "I suppose I'm not in any position to complain about that. If it wasn't for my initial deception, you wouldn't have had to send that letter." Then his brow furrowed. "But why did you go to such lengths to find the owner? I know that you like to trace the origins of your antiques, but that seems a bit extreme..."

"Even for me?" Sadie said with a smile, finishing his sentence. "You're right. It was. Poor Val was almost shaking when we met and she recognized me. She told me everything and even took me to her dorm room, where I met her roommate, May, and May's brother, Alex."

His gaze narrowed, a curious gleam in his eyes as he picked up his mug. "Now I know there's more to it."

Sadie took another sip of her coffee, knowing that the time had come to spill everything. She set down her mug and met Alfred's gaze. "I was arrested for possession of stolen property. And that property was inside your Steiff teddy bear."

Alfred almost dropped his coffee mug, a splash of the dark brew spilling on the table in front of him. But he ignored it, his face pale with shock. "What?"

His shocked reaction told Sadie that he couldn't have anything to do with the coin in the teddy bear. Relief flowed through her. When he'd first told her about his bad investment, she'd almost been afraid he'd done something drastic—something even criminal. She should have known better—but there were too many stories in history of good men making bad decisions in a moment of panic.

And Alfred Daly was a good man.

"Sadie, you can't be serious," Alfred said, still oblivious to the spilled coffee in front of him.

"I'm afraid I am." She rose from the table and retrieved a paper towel from the kitchen counter. Walking over to Alfred's side of the table, she began to wipe up the spill. "I was arrested at the Antique Mine two days after the Ferris estate auction."

"But it makes no sense," Alfred said as she dropped the paper towel in the trash can and returned to the table. "How in the world would stolen property get inside my teddy bear? And what was it?"

"It was a Huntley silver dollar."

He blanched, then slowly shook his head. "How is that even possible?"

"I thought you might be able to tell me."

He stared at her for a long moment. Then a smile curved his mouth. "Well, I'm very happy to say that I have no idea how the Huntley coin got there."

"Of course you don't," Sadie said with a sigh of relief. Her instincts had been right about Alfred after all. "You know, I saw some of Huntley's silver work at the American Mining Museum. It was exquisite."

"But how did the police know a Huntley silver dollar was in the teddy bear?"

Sadie told him about the anonymous tip the police received, and how Giselle had purchased the teddy bear the day after the auction, and how Spike had seen a blonde woman toss the teddy bear over the back fence at the Antique Mine shortly before the police arrived.

By the time she was through, Alfred was shaking his head in disbelief. "So it seems that someone is trying to frame you. The question is who and why?"

"I don't know if they're trying to frame me personally, or if they would have done this to whoever had bought the teddy bear that day. But something's not right."

He leaned forward. "Please tell me how I can help you."

"You already have," she said gently. "Just knowing you're in my corner helps more than you know." Then she decided to go one step further and give him some unsolicited advice. "You should tell Cecile, you know. She'll understand."

He sighed. "I know. I've tried more times than I care to admit. I just dread seeing the disappointment in her eyes."

"She loves you, Alfred," Sadie reminded him. "For better or for worse, remember?"

He nodded. "And for richer or poorer. Unfortunately, it looks like we're headed for poorer."

"Have faith," she told him.

Sadie's phone buzzed. She looked down to read a text on her screen. "It's Brent Fielder. I'd called him earlier this morning, but it went to voice mail. I left my name and number and said I'd like to meet with him. He just texted me back and wrote that he'll be available at ten o'clock this morning, followed by his address."

Alfred glanced up at the cuckoo clock. "It's close to ten now." Then he frowned. "Does Fielder know you've been charged in connection with his stolen Huntley coins?"

"I have no idea," she said. "When I left the message, I didn't mention anything about that." Sadie knew she couldn't pass up this opportunity. She drained her coffee mug and then rose from her chair. "I hate to leave on such short notice, but if I go now, I can just make it there by ten o'clock."

"Why don't I come with you?" Alfred suggested.

Sadie considered the offer. "Don't you have class?"

"I can skip it," he said with a wry smile. "My students would probably be thrilled."

But Sadie didn't want to pull him away from his classes. "I appreciate the offer, but it might be better if I meet with Brent alone. I'll let you know what happens."

"Okay," he said with a nod. Then he walked over to Sadie. "Are we good?"

She reached out to give him a hug. "Yes, we're good. Tell Cecile hello for me."

"I will," he promised. "I'll tell her everything."

Sadie smiled to herself as he escorted her to the front door, so happy that she'd faced her fear and gone to Alfred for the truth.

Now it was time to see what truths Brent Fielder could tell her.

The Fielder mansion was located in the prestigious Shock Hill neighborhood of Breckenridge. The long, paved driveway was edged with large boulders on either side, and the three-story house boasted a six-car garage. Huge windows stretched from the ground floor to the peaked roof.

Sadie parked her Tahoe and walked to the front door. She rang the doorbell, surprised that Mr. Fielder didn't have a gated entrance like so many of the other grand houses in the area.

A few moments later, a woman in her midthirties answered the door. She was dressed in a traditional maid's uniform, from the tips of her sensible black shoes to the white cap on top of her head.

"May I help you?" the maid asked.

"I'm Sadie Speers. I believe Mr. Fielder is expecting me."

The maid nodded and opened the door wide enough for Sadie to enter. "Yes, he is. Please come in, Ms. Speers."

Sadie walked into the grand foyer and peered up at the vaulted ceiling. A chandelier, bigger than her kitchen table, hung there, the crystals dangling from it catching the sunlight that streamed in through the large window.

"This way, please," the maid said, and started walking through the wide foyer.

Sadie followed her, trying to keep up as she took in the layout of the mansion and the hundreds of historical artifacts and vintage collectibles in every direction. Some of them were displayed in glass cases or buffets, but others had been made part of the eclectic decor, which varied from stark modernism to Victorian fussiness—and everything in between.

Sadie soon realized that she'd be unable to find her way back to the foyer as she followed the maid through a maze of hallways. Finally, they stopped at a pair of double oak doors. The maid opened one of them and ushered Sadie inside. "Mr. Fielder will be with you shortly. May I get you anything while you wait?"

"No, I'm fine. Thank you."

The maid nodded before leaving the room and closing the door behind her.

Sadie stood alone in the grand room, which looked as if had been taken straight out of a Victorian parlor. There was a baby grand piano on one side of the room, along with a harp on a stand. The cozy sitting area had antique, red-velvet furniture and a coffee table sporting an antique china tea set on a silver tray. Along each wall were glass display cases.

Sadie began at one end of the room and slowly made her way to the other side, looking at the wide variety of collections. There were thimble collections, sets of cutlery in both silver and gold, a collection of vintage handkerchiefs and neckties, along with several old books, most of them bound in calfskin. Along with the books were a wide assortment of antique quills and inkpots.

The door opened behind her and she turned to see a man, who appeared to be about forty years old, enter the room. He was tall and handsome, with dark hair and eyes. His lips were thin and pale beneath a finely trimmed black mustache.

"You must be Ms. Speers," he said, advancing toward her with both arms outstretched. "I'm Brent Fielder." He clasped both of her hands in his when he reached her and gave them each a hearty shake. "So nice of you to come here."

"Thank you for inviting me," she said, a little taken aback by his gregarious nature after Val's description of him.

"It's my pleasure. I don't often have the opportunity to meet someone who has outsmarted my security system."

She blinked. "Excuse me?"

He smiled. "My private investigator told me you were found with one of my Huntley silver dollars and have been charged in the matter."

"Private investigator?" Sadie echoed, wondering if he could be the anonymous tipster. Could he also have planted the GPS tracker in the mystery box?

"Well, that's what he calls himself, but the fact that he only found out about your arrest after you left your voice mail message this morning showed me how worthless he really is. He's been fired, so it no longer matters." Then he motioned to the red-velvet settee. "Please, have a seat."

For a moment, Sadie wondered if Brent Fielder was quite sane. He seemed unusually cheerful about meeting the person he believed had stolen one of his Huntley coins. She walked over to the settee and settled onto the padded cushion.

"Now," he said, taking a seat in one of the wing chairs across from her, "I assume you've come here to plead for mercy. Well, I'm happy to give it, but I'm afraid the criminal charges are out of my hands."

Sadie held up one hand. "There's seems to be a big misunderstanding, Mr. Fielder. I..."

"Call me Brent," he said with a smile.

"Okay, Brent. I didn't steal the Huntley coin," Sadie said evenly. "And I certainly didn't break in to your house. I believe someone tried to frame me for the crime, however, and I was hoping you might be able to help me figure out who that person might be."

His brow furrowed. "But you were charged, right?"

"Yes, with possession of stolen property. One of the Huntley coins was found in a Steiff teddy bear that I purchased at the Ferris estate auction. But only one."

"Only one!" He smiled broadly. "My private investigator didn't tell me that."

Sadie stared at him. "I didn't expect you to be so happy about it."

He leaned forward in the chair. "Sadie...may I call you by your first name?"

"Of course."

"What do you know about Eustace Huntley?"

"Not much, I'm afraid," she said. "I've done a little research on him, but there's not much out there that I can find."

He slapped his hands on his knees. "Well, then you've come to the right place, because I make it my business to know the pedigree of my collections."

Sadie sat back, both surprised and entertained by the man known as the King of Fakes. "I'd love to hear about the Huntley pedigree."

"Then you shall." He cleared his throat. "Eustace Huntley was the black sheep of the Huntley family. Hardly surprising, since Eustace was in prison for so many years."

"After he was caught using his counterfeit silver dollars?"

Brent nodded. "Which meant he was swindling friends and neighbors and even his fellow church members in Silver Peak." He tilted his head to one side. "You're from there, I believe."

"Yes, I am. But I'm not familiar with any families named Huntley."

"That's probably because they all moved out of the state shortly after Eustace was sent to prison. He was actually arrested on the eve of his wedding to Nora Primm, a member of a very prominent family in Silver Peak. Apparently, she was the only one who stood by him after his arrest and visited him regularly at the state penitentiary after his conviction, although they never married."

Sadie could well imagine the scandal. "What happened after he got out of prison?"

"He caught the Spanish flu in 1918 and died alone." Brent sighed. "Some said the scoundrel got what he deserved, but judging by his work, Huntley was quite talented as a silversmith."

"Yes, I saw some of his work at the American Mining Museum. It's too bad he used his talent for greed instead of good."

"But it's a great story, isn't it?" Brent said with a smile. "It has everything—greed, betrayal, loyalty, and even politics."

"Politics?" Sadie echoed.

He nodded. "The scandal happened right before Eustace Huntley's brother was to officially declare his run for governor of Colorado. He was an odds-on favorite to win too. Eustace changed history—and that's why those Huntley silver dollars are so valuable among certain collectors today."

Sadie appreciated hearing the story, but she had one question for Brent. "So why are you happy that only one of the Huntley silver dollars has been found?"

"Well, Sadie, as I'm sure you know, I love collecting rare objects. There are only ten Huntley counterfeit silver coins in existence, so they're very rare. And because of that, they are very well insured. In fact, they're insured for well over the current market price, so it's really a win-win for me. I'll have at least one of the Huntley coins back in my possession, and I'll receive a nice fat check for the other nine coins."

"I see." His answer made Sadie wonder if Brent might be responsible for the theft of his own coins.

He breathed a wistful sigh. "You know, as much as the story of Eustace Huntley intrigues me, I have to admit that the romantic angle is my favorite part of the story. His bride-to-be vowed to wait until he was released from prison to marry him. Unfortunately, he died before they could wed, as so many people did back then."

Brent jumped up from his chair and walked quickly toward one of the glass display cases. "In fact, I have her journal. I tracked it down after acquiring all ten of the Huntley coins."

He turned and flashed a smile at Sadie. "I guess that's just the romantic side in me. Plus, I thought there might be more value in including the journal with the Huntley coins if I ever decided to sell them all as a set."

He opened the glass case and carefully pulled out one of the calfskin books. After opening the front cover, he nodded. "Yes, this is the one."

He brought it over to the settee and handed it to Sadie. "Would you like to take a peek?"

"I would," she said, intrigued. The book was a little fragile, so she handled it with great care as she lifted the front cover and saw a name inscribed on the first page: *Private Diary of Miss Nora Primm.*

The word *private* was underlined twice.

"She certainly had fine penmanship," Brent said, looking at the book over Sadie's shoulder. "Well, they all did back then, it seems. Nothing better to do back in the olden days than practice their penmanship, I guess."

Sadie rose to her feet. "Brent, would you mind if I borrowed this diary? I promise to take excellent care of it."

He hesitated a moment and then shrugged his shoulders. "Sure, why not? You own an antique shop, right? So I'm sure you'll treat it right. Besides, now that most of the Huntley coins are gone, the journal is really of no value to me."

"Thank you," she said, tucking the diary carefully into her purse before he changed his mind. "By the way, do you remember a woman by the name of Valerie Nichols? I believe she attended your most recent seminar."

He pursed his lips, appearing deep in thought, but finally shook his head. "Sorry, but the name doesn't ring a bell."

"She's pursuing a master's degree in history at Colorado Mountain College," Sadie said, hoping to prod his memory. "I believe she asked you a question about lending some of your antiques to museums."

Brent thoughtfully tapped his chin with one finger. "Sorry, I really can't remember her. I see so many people and answer so many questions. I guess they all just blur together after a while."

Sadie found that a little hard to believe, but then Brent himself was a little hard to believe. "I should be on my way. Thank you so much for your time."

"You're welcome," he said. "And good luck at your trial." He walked over and pressed a button on the wall. "The maid will show you out. Have a nice day."

Sadie watched as he left the room, leaving the door open behind him. She could hear him whistling a jaunty tune as he walked down the marble hallway.

The maid appeared a moment later and escorted Sadie to the front door. Brent Fielder hadn't helped her find the culprit, but he'd revealed something of himself. Perhaps his private investigator had planted that Huntley coin and the GPS tracker in the mystery box she'd purchased for Roz. That way Brent could turn in a claim for nine stolen Huntley coins and keep one, legitimately, for himself. As for the others, he'd probably be able to find a way to sell them on the black market.

It was a theory, anyway, to go along with all the others. Sadie breathed a deep sigh as she walked to her Tahoe. A new theory wouldn't stop her upcoming evidentiary hearing, which was scheduled for one week from today.

She needed to find evidence to prove her innocence, and she needed to find it fast.

15

After returning home from Breckenridge, Sadie carried Nora Primm's diary out onto the front porch and sat in the rocking chair. She'd enjoyed an early lunch of leftover tuna casserole and a salad, her thoughts still on the odd encounter she'd had with Brent Fielder.

She planned to go to the Antique Mine soon, but she wanted to take a sneak peek at Nora Primm's diary first. She wasn't even sure what she was searching for, but the fact that Brent had pointed it out to her might mean something.

Hank lay curled on the front step, his eyelids drooping as a fly buzzed around his head.

Sadie carefully opened the front cover of the diary and then turned past the first page. That's when she noticed that several pages had been torn out. She wondered if Nora had feared that she'd revealed too much of her private thoughts or had simply been embarrassed by them. As she flipped to the first entry, Sadie began to read.

November 1, 1903

Silver Peak, Colorado

Dear Diary,

I turn eighteen years old tomorrow and leave the cares of youth behind me. Mother wants me to learn to manage a household, as there are several young suitors eager to court me. I have no use for them as long as HE lives in this world. HE is strong and handsome. HE is the perfect man for me in every way except one. Yes, dear diary, he is a poor man. This is through no fault of his own. His father is a wastrel and spends too much time with his books. But HE is wonderful, and we steal away together whenever possible. I have become an avid walker and take long hikes in the woods. Mother fears the sun shall brown my skin, but I take great care to stay in the shade. HE is all the sun I need.

Sadie smiled to herself as she came to the end of the entry. The more things changed, the more they stayed the same. A young girl in love, so certain that the man of her dreams was perfect for her. Times were different then, Sadie thought to herself. Women had few options other than marriage, though Colorado had seen its share of independent women homesteaders and business owners.

But it seemed Nora Primm had already set her sights on a man by her eighteenth birthday. Sadie turned the page, wondering if that man was Eustace Huntley. She promised herself she'd only read one more entry before heading into town.

November 4, 1903
Silver Peak, Colorado

Dear Diary,

Mother and Father are bickering again. At times, I find it hard to believe that they were ever in love. Mother claims Father became smitten with her at sixteen and brought her flowers every day of their courtship. Today, they were bickering over wildflowers that I had picked on my walk in the woods. Mother thinks it is unseemly for me to walk without a chaperone. Father says it is good for a girl to get some exercise and that perhaps Mother should be my chaperone, especially since she is so fond of the fairy cakes that Cook makes.

I shall never bicker with E. I shall cherish E. and make him happy each and every day. I count every moment until I can see him again and dream of what we shall say to each other. E. told me that he wants to leave the ranch and find a job in town. Perhaps Father can help him, although I must be cautious and not reveal too much. If Father knew about E., he would send me away to Aunt Lydia's place in Omaha and I have no desire to live with a spinster aunt who smells of mothballs. I have other plans for my life.

I shall wait until Father is in good spirits and find a way to persuade him to help E. He always gives me what I want.

Now it seemed obvious to Sadie that *E.* stood for Eustace. It saddened her a little to already know the fate of the two young sweethearts. She closed the diary with a wistful sigh and placed it back in the protective plastic bag she'd decided to keep it in. That way it would stay in good condition until she could return it to Brent Fielder.

Sadie rose from the rocking chair, the movement waking Hank from his nap. He followed her into the house and headed for the rug in front of the fireplace to resume his nap while Sadie got ready to go into town.

Twenty minutes later, Sadie walked into the Antique Mine. Julie stood behind the front counter while chatting with a customer whom Sadie didn't recognize. She greeted them both and then headed into the back room.

After her eventful morning, a feeling of peace washed over her now that she was back in her shop. She walked over to the silver tray that she was restoring for Harry Polmiller, running one finger over the polished, shiny center. Then she pushed up the sleeves of her blue polo shirt and set to work on it once more.

She began to hum along as "Amazing Grace" played over the music speakers in the shop, her fingers slowly working the polishing cloth over the platter. No matter what happened in the coming weeks, she knew the Lord would be with her. Sadie dabbed the cloth into the polishing compound and applied it to the platter, thrilled to see the tarnish fade away to reveal the silver underneath.

Footsteps sounded behind her. Sadie turned to see Julie in the room.

"Sorry to interrupt," Julie said with a smile. "I love this hymn."

"Me too." Sadie set down the cloth and then wiped her hands with a clean towel. "How's business today?"

"It's been nice and steady. I sold some vintage cookbooks to the woman who was just here. She's from California and visiting friends in the area." Julie walked over for a better view of the platter. "That's coming along nicely. Harry won't even recognize it when it's done."

Sadie smiled. "It's gorgeous, isn't it?"

"It sure is." Then Julie looked over at her. "Do you plan to be here awhile?"

"Most of the afternoon," Sadie said. "Do you need to go?"

Julie nodded. "Just for an hour or so. I have to mail a package to my sister. My husband was supposed to do it, but he called earlier to tell me he forgot it at home."

"Go ahead," Sadie urged her. "And take your time."

Julie smiled. "Thanks." She was almost out the door when she turned back. "Oh, I meant to tell you. I set those pamphlets out by the front door. I hope that's all right."

Sadie nodded, having almost forgotten about the tourist attraction pamphlets that had been in Roz's mystery box. "Yes, that's fine. Thank you."

Julie waved to her and then disappeared into the main part of the shop. Sadie stepped out just in time to watch her leave. The aroma of coffee from Arbuckle's drifted into the Antique Mine, tempting Sadie into walking over to order a cup.

To her surprise, Roz was standing at the counter, chatting with Luz Arbuckle. "Sadie," Roz exclaimed when she saw her. "I was just coming to see you."

Luz chuckled. "I call that perfect timing." She handed two cups to Roz. "Here's your order. Enjoy!"

"Thanks." Roz turned to Sadie and handed her a cup. "This one's for you."

Sadie smiled. "You read my mind."

"That's what happens when you know someone for so long," Roz said, winking playfully at Luz.

Roz wore a long red tunic sweater over a pair of blue jeans. Her brown, fringed leather boots came up all the way to her knees.

And around her neck, Roz wore the beaded peace symbol neck-lace that she'd found in the mystery box.

"I love your outfit," Sadie told her as they walked into the Antique Mine through the open doorway separating the two shops. "What did Roscoe think of your purchase?"

"He grumbled about it," she said with a chuckle. "But then he spent half a day paging through that old Sears and Roebuck cata-log and comparing how the cost of tools has changed since then."

Sadie smiled. "My guess is that they were better tools and cost less."

"That's what he said," Roz chimed. She hitched herself up on a stool next to the front counter and set her cup on the marble top. "Now, tell me what's happening with you. Anything new on the teddy bear front?"

Sadie sighed, hardly knowing where to start. First, she told Roz about her meeting with Val and the girl's guilt over taking the teddy bear to her dorm room the weekend before the auction. That led to revealing that Alfred had owned the Steiff bear she'd purchased at the estate auction, but Sadie didn't discuss his money problems. Lastly, she described her meeting with Brent Fielder earlier today.

"That Fielder fellow sounds a bit loony," Roz said after Sadie finished her story.

"I think he's just eccentric," Sadie replied. "And very focused on the value of things. When I asked him about Val, who had attended his seminar, he seemed completely unaware of her exis-tence. It's almost as if things and people have no meaning to him outside of their value. I think the only reason he seemed happy to meet me was the fact that he thought I'd stolen his coins and he'd make more money collecting the insurance on them then if he'd sold them." Sadie paused. "Although he did seem quite enamored of the Eustace Huntley story."

"Maybe he staged their disappearance," Roz ventured. "Just to collect that insurance money. And then planted the coin in the Steiff bear to make you—or whoever bought it—look guilty and take the attention off of him."

That thought had occurred to Sadie too, though she had dismissed it. "I suppose it's possible, but how would he have had the opportunity to plant the coin in the bear? And if he still had the coins in his possession, I don't think he would have given me the diary."

Roz blinked. "You didn't say anything about a diary."

There had been so much to tell about her meetings with Val, Alfred, and Brent, that she realized she'd left out one of the most interesting parts. "Brent had a diary that belonged to Eustace Huntley's fiancée. Her name was Nora Primm, and she stood by him through his arrest and conviction, although they never married. I don't think Brent would have let me borrow the diary if he had the set of Huntley coins intact. Now that nine of them are gone, the diary has no value to him."

"Well, then he is an odd duck," Roz said. "So have you read the diary?"

"I started reading it after lunch. Nora was eighteen and secretly courting a boy her parents didn't think was worthy of her."

"Star-crossed lovers," Roz said with a sigh. "Too bad we already know how their love story turned out."

"I may have a love story happening under my roof too." Sadie told Roz about Sara's lie about Tre and her odd behavior of late.

Roz smiled. "Well, Grandma, it seems her visit is a little more exciting than you bargained for."

"I'll say," Sadie agreed. "I'd almost forgotten how much work teenagers can be."

Roz nodded and then took a sip of her coffee. "Speaking of love," she said with a mischievous smile. "Where is Edwin taking you for your birthday on Saturday?"

Sadie gave a small shrug. "Actually, he hasn't invited me anywhere. He may too busy to get together."

"Too busy?" Roz said in disbelief. "Nonsense!"

"He's working on a project to restore some of the vacant Victorian houses in town. To tell you the truth, I think my birthday may have slipped his mind."

"Well, then," Roz said, "you're invited to my house for dinner on Saturday night. I'll be making all of your favorites."

Sadie smiled, holding up one hand. "Whoa, there. You don't have to do that."

"I *want* to do it," Roz insisted. "We'll have so much fun. And Edwin is invited, of course. It's been a while since the four of us have spent an evening together."

"It does sound fun."

"Good!" Roz grinned, rubbing her hands together. "I'm going to create the menu this afternoon and go grocery shopping."

Before Sadie could reply, two elderly women entered the shop. Sadie rounded the front counter to greet them. "Good afternoon. May I help you find something?"

"Oh, we just stopped by to browse," said one of the women. "We're from Denver and every once in a while we take a day trip and go antiquing. We've never been to your shop before. It looks quite nice."

Sadie smiled. "Well, thank you. Just let me know if you need any help."

"We will," they both replied at the same time.

Sadie returned to the front counter, where Roz was hitching her purse strap over her shoulder.

"I'd better go now that I have plans for the afternoon," Roz said.

"Is there anything you want me to bring on Saturday?"

Roz shook her head as she headed for the door. "Just your boyfriend and a big appetite."

Sadie grinned, waving to her best friend. "I think I can manage that."

Later that afternoon, Sadie drove her Tahoe to the high school to pick up Sara. She arrived early, planning to surprise her granddaughter so she didn't have to take the school bus to Sadie's house. She even planned to stop for ice-cream sundaes on the way home.

But as Sadie approached the high school, she was surprised to see the parking lot was almost empty. Only two cars remained, and one of them was parked in the principal's designated spot.

Sadie parked her car and walked inside the high school. The halls were empty too, and the building oddly quiet. She approached the principal's office and saw the secretary behind the glass wall, seated at her desk and typing on the computer keyboard in front of her. Sadie tapped on the door.

The secretary looked up and waved her in. "Hello, Sadie. What brings you here?"

"My granddaughter," Sadie told her. "I decided to pick Sara up from school, but nobody seems to be here."

The secretary's forehead crinkled in confusion. "The school let out at two o'clock today for a teachers' meeting. Didn't Sara tell you?"

"No," Sadie said, trying to hide her surprise. "She must have forgotten to say something."

The secretary flashed a smile. "Typical teenager, I guess."

"Yes," Sadie said, nodding. "Thanks for your help."

"Anytime," the secretary said, returning to her computer as Sadie walked out of the office.

It was possible that Sara had forgotten to tell her about the early dismissal, Sadie thought to herself. The girl had probably taken the bus to Sadie's house and was there right at this moment. But the sinking feeling in pit of Sadie's stomach told her otherwise.

When she reached the parking lot, Sadie dialed Sara's cell phone number. After one ring, her granddaughter's phone instantly went to voice mail, so Sadie left a message. "Hi, Sara, this is Grandma. Please give me a call when you get a chance."

Then Sadie called her home phone. It rang four times, but Sara never picked up. Sadie disconnected the phone, the sinking feeling growing even stronger inside of her.

She climbed into her Tahoe and then glanced at her watch. It was almost half past three, which meant that Sara had been out of school for ninety minutes.

But where would she go?

Home. That thought came unbidden to her mind, but Sadie knew it was the first place she should check. Alice had given a spare house key to both Sara and Theo shortly after they'd all moved to Silver Peak. Perhaps Sara had simply wanted to check on the house and make sure everything was all right.

But why hadn't she called so Sadie wouldn't worry? Unless she'd purposely kept the information about the early dismissal from Sadie. Another lie of omission, perhaps? Sadie shook off that thought, torn between worry and frustration. "It shouldn't be this difficult to keep track of a fourteen-year-old girl," she said out loud, pulling out of the high school parking lot.

Sadie drove straight to Alice's house, taking care not to exceed the speed limit in her haste to get there. She wasn't sure where to look next if she didn't find Sara there. Mia was always a possibility, but she hated to contact the Garza family again in search of her granddaughter. "Oh, Alice," she murmured as she drove, "you can't come home soon enough for me."

When she turned the last corner, Sadie saw a pickup truck parked in front of Alice's house. A blue pickup.

The same blue pickup that Tre Havelock had driven when he'd dropped Sara off at Sadie's house just yesterday.

Sadie's frustration turned to anger as she pulled into the driveway and then switched off the engine. She couldn't believe that girl would bring a boy to her empty house.

A seventeen-year-old boy!

Sadie marched up to the front door and tried to turn the knob, but it was locked. She dug inside her purse for the key, the process taking longer than she wanted. At last, she found it and unlocked the door.

As the door swung open, she heard Sara call out, "It's my grandma! Hide!"

Even with all the emotions swirling around inside her, Sadie couldn't help but smile at the absurdity of it all. Did Sara forget that Tre's pickup truck was right outside? Did she truly think Sadie wouldn't hear her telling him to hide?

Sadie stepped over the threshold. "Sara Louise Macomb, you come out here right now." The sternness in her tone even scared Sadie a little.

So it was no surprise that when Sara emerged from the office off the living room, that she looked as white as a ghost. "Hey, Grandma."

"Where's Tre?" Sadie asked her.

Sara hitched her thumb over her shoulder. "Um, he's fixing something on the computer. I asked him if he could just come over for a minute..."

A teenage boy emerged from the office. He was tall and lanky, with a mop of shaggy blond hair that hung over half his face. He reached up to brush it away and then said, "Hey, I'm Tre. You must be Sara's grandma."

"Hello, Tre," Sadie said, trying to keep her voice calm. "It's nice to meet you, but I'm afraid Sara isn't allowed to have guests here when her mother is away."

"Understandable," Tre said, his hair flopping back over his face. He started toward the door. "See ya later, Sara."

"'Bye," Sara said weakly, not meeting Sadie's gaze.

Sadie stepped out of the doorway so Tre could leave, almost choking a little at the strong scent of his cologne. When the door closed behind him, Sadie turned to her granddaughter.

"Well, young lady," Sadie said, sounding eerily like her own mother, "what do you have to say for yourself?"

16

"I've never been so embarrassed in my life!"

Those were the only words Sara said to Sadie after leaving Alice's house and heading home.

Sara climbed out of the car and stomped toward the front porch. She stood with her arms folded together and waited by the door for Sadie to unlock it.

"Sara, we need to talk about this," Sadie said calmly. Her own anger had cooled in the interim, and she just wanted her granddaughter to understand how inappropriate it was to invite a seventeen-year-old boy to her house when no one else was at home.

"You just don't understand, Grandma," Sara whined, stomping one foot on the wood floor.

Sadie pushed the door open and Sara ran into the living room and headed straight for the stairs, taking them two at a time to the second floor. Moments later, Sadie heard a door slam.

She sighed. "Teenagers."

If she'd learned anything in her sixty-two years, it was timing. Sara needed time to cool off and realize that her world wasn't ending. Being embarrassed by a parent or grandparent was a rite of passage for every teenage boy and girl. The fact that Sara was in the wrong would have to be pointed out later for it to finally sink in.

Her gaze fell on the diary on the dining room table. Needing some time of her own to unwind, Sadie picked up the diary and removed it from the plastic bag before carrying it over to the living room. Hank stood at the foot of the staircase, staring up at the empty landing.

"Come here, boy," she called to him, patting her leg. "Sara needs some alone-time."

Hank jumped up on the sofa and waited for Sadie to sit down before he settled himself on the cushion beside her and rested his head on her lap.

Sadie opened the diary to the place she'd left off and began to read, one hand gently petting Hank's silky neck.

November 19, 1903
Silver Peak, Colorado

Dear Diary,

Lila May saw us in the woods. I told E. to hide, but he walked straight up to her and introduced himself. She acted like a ninny, but I could see her sly looks toward me. Now Mother and Father will find out, since Lila May has a tongue like a serpent.

I shall have to pretend to break it off with E. before Father confronts him and ruins everything. So much care is required in all this planning that I have begun to suffer headaches. Mother doses me with headache powder, but the only way to ease the pain is to lie in a quiet, dark room until the headache subsides.

That may work in my favor. Patience is the key.

I shall start locking my bedroom door during my headaches. It shall be easy enough to slip out after dusk and meet E. to resume our courtship. He may balk, of course, at my unladylike behavior, but I shall not be dissuaded. My very happiness is at stake.

Sadie breathed a wistful sigh as she turned the page, realizing that teenage girls had schemed to meet the boy of their dreams even back then. She felt a moment of compassion for Nora's poor parents and wondered how they'd felt when they'd learned their daughter was engaged to a criminal.

Curious to see how it unfolded, Sadie began to read the next entry.

January 3, 1904

Silver Peak, Colorado

Dear Diary,

The winter days drag by with nothing to do but draw or sew or take tea. I miss E. so much, but the snow prevents our meetings in the woods. I must have patience. My headaches occur daily, or so I claim, and I retire to my room by early evening and lock the door. When spring arrives, they will be none the wiser when I open the window and flee this house.

I received a letter from Lila May. She is recuperating at a hospital in Arizona after stepping on a wasps' nest. Silly girl probably didn't hear the buzzing with all her talking. Everyone gets their due in time.

Patience is the key. Sometimes I want to scream at the idle days that consume me. But when the snow clears and the weather warms, it will be a time for new beginnings.

Sadie closed the diary, a little disturbed by this latest entry. Had Nora actually written that Lila May deserved to be swarmed by wasps? A knock at the front door broke her reverie and caused Hank to leap from the sofa and emit one soft bark. Then he trotted over to the door, his tail wagging.

Sadie opened the door and saw Edwin standing on the other side. "Hello," she said with a smile. "This is a nice surprise."

Edwin smiled. "I hope I'm not catching you at a bad time."

Sadie glanced toward the stairs. Since she still hadn't heard a peep from Sara, she stepped out on the porch, closing the door behind her. "Not at all. What brings you here?"

"Both business and pleasure," he said, then his gaze narrowed. "Something's bothering you, Sadie. What is it?"

"Well, I caught Sara alone at Alice's house with a boy. A seventeen-year-old boy."

Concern flashed in his eyes. "Is she all right?"

"Oh, she's fine," Sadie said. "More embarrassed than anything. I don't think she liked the way I reacted in front of Tre."

He blinked. "Tre Havelock?"

"Yes. Do you know him?"

Edwin hesitated for a moment. "Well, in a way. His parents approached me a few weeks ago about possibly purchasing one of the Victorian houses the town plans to restore. They're renting a house at the moment, but they want to set down roots here."

"I'm starting to wish they hadn't moved here at all," Sadie said, and then waved away her comment. "Don't listen to me. I'm just upset with Sara's behavior lately. I'd been so looking forward to her staying with me, and it's just not happening the way I'd imagined."

He cocked his head to one side. "Surely, it isn't that bad?"

"Well, no," she admitted. "We've had some good times. It's just this boy that's been causing some trouble."

"You know how teenagers are," Edwin said with a wink. She felt her cheeks flush, thinking about how they themselves had been high school sweethearts. "I'm sure it will pass."

"I hope you're right." Then she motioned to the chairs on the porch. "Let's sit down. May I get you something to drink?"

"No, thanks. I'm fine." Edwin took a seat in one of the porch chairs and Sadie did the same.

The afternoon sun shone brightly, and the clear, blue sky provided a perfect backdrop for the mountains around them. Sadie breathed in a deep breath of fresh air, ready to enjoy some time with Edwin. "So business or pleasure? Which shall we talk about first?"

He smiled. "Lady's choice."

"Okay, then let's start with pleasure."

He leaned forward in the chair. "Well, you have a birthday coming up, so I'd like to invite you for an evening of dinner and dancing."

"That sounds delightful," she said, smiling. "But I'm afraid I've already accepted a dinner invitation on my birthday."

His face fell. "Oh?"

Her smile widened. "Roz invited both of us to dinner at her house on Saturday night and I already accepted. I hope you don't mind."

"Mind?" he said, chuckling. "I'm relieved. For a moment there, I was afraid I had some competition."

"Well, you never know," she said playfully. "I did meet an unusual man in Breckenridge this morning, although I don't think he's my type."

"And who was that?"

Sadie filled him in on her meeting with Brent Fielder and what she'd learned about him and his collections. She also told him about Nora Primm's diary and the entries about Nora's infatuation with a boy named E. "I'm sure the *E.* stands for Eustace. She seemed quite smitten with him, although..."

"Yes?" Edwin prodded.

"Well, her last entry was a little...strange. Of course, I could be reading it wrong. I'll let you know when I get further along."

He nodded. "It sounds intriguing. Let me know what happens."

"I will," she promised. "Now, how about telling me that business that brought you here?"

His smile faded. "Well, Sadie, I think we should talk about your hearing that's scheduled for next week."

His words were like a bucket of cold water. "I suppose we should."

"I just want you to know what to expect. This isn't a trial, mind you, but rather the next step in the process. The prosecutor will show any evidence that you committed a crime, and the judge will decide if it's enough evidence for you to go to trial. I'll be there to assist you as defense counsel, of course."

She met his gaze. "And you're still sure you want to do that?"

"You couldn't keep me away," he said softly.

Sadie appreciated his support, especially after her earlier fears that he was pulling away from her. Still, she hated the thought of going to court next Monday and of Edwin having to defend her against a crime she didn't commit.

"I need to find Giselle," Sadie said at last. "She must be the key to all of this. Someone sent her to buy that bear—or she's the culprit herself. One way or the other, I have to track her down."

"Any possible leads?" he asked.

Sadie shook her head. "Not yet. I've called every modeling agency around and searched a phone directory during my trips to Breckenridge. My Internet searches haven't turned up anything about her either. It's obvious now that Giselle Fleur was an alias she used so that no one could find her."

"We'll get through this, Sadie," Edwin said firmly. "If this ridiculous case goes to trial, I'll have enough character witnesses lined up that it will take a full week to get through them all."

She knew those words were meant to make her feel better, but she didn't want to drag her friends and neighbors into this mess. The sooner she could put it behind her, the better. "We've still got a week to find something to clear me."

He gave her an encouraging smile. "And if anyone can do that, I know you can."

The next day, Sadie spent the morning tidying up the Antique Mine and helping customers. Every once in a while, she'd steal away to the back room to work on Harry's silver tray. It was almost finished now, and she couldn't wait to show it to him.

Sara had finally come downstairs last evening to join Sadie for supper. Thankfully, the girl's mood had improved and she'd apologized to Sadie for her behavior. They'd ended the meal with a hug and chocolate pudding. Then Sara had returned to her bedroom to finish her homework while Sadie had perused more of Nora's diary.

The entries she'd read last night mostly chronicled the boring winter days Nora endured until she could see her beloved E. again. Her headaches hadn't abated, although she'd learned that dabbing her temples with cold vinegar did help lessen the ache.

A call from Alice had ended Sadie's reading for the night, and she'd carefully explained Sara's latest escapade with Tre, making certain to assure Alice that everything was under control. To Sadie's surprise and relief, Alice wasn't as upset as she'd expected.

And Sadie had made it clear to Sara at breakfast this morning that she wasn't to be alone with Tre again—in his pickup truck or anywhere else. Now she just hoped her lovestruck granddaughter would be strong enough to follow through.

Sadie walked around the shop, taking stock of her inventory and wondering what else she should do until lunch. Her gaze fell on the pile of pamphlets that Julie had put on the pedestal table near the front door. They'd been picked through and now sat askew on the green marble tabletop. Sadie gathered them together and then neatly fanned them apart so at least a portion of the titles and cover photos were visible.

Then her eye caught something familiar. Or rather, *someone*. Sadie pulled the pamphlet for Carter Park, which featured the side profiles of three people—two women and a man—climbing an indoor rock wall.

Unless Sadie's eyes were deceiving her, she'd say one of those women was Giselle. She pulled the pamphlet from the stack, realizing she'd never really looked closely at any of them before now.

As she stared at the woman's profile on the cover, she couldn't be sure it was the same woman who had purchased the Steiff teddy bear. The long legs, skin tone, and dark hair definitely matched Giselle, but only a small portion of her face was visible in the photograph.

Sadie began flipping through the pages, searching for more pictures. If Giselle had told the truth about working as a model, perhaps she'd been hired for a photo shoot to promote Carter Park.

She found a photograph of the same three rock wall climbers in the middle of the pamphlet. Only in this picture they were skating at the Carter Park ice rink. This time, the woman was facing the camera. Sadie studied the photograph.

Same smile. Same eyes. Same tiny beauty mark near the corner of her mouth.

She'd found Giselle.

Sadie hurried over to the front counter and picked up the phone, quickly punching in Julie's number on the dial pad. She hated to ask her to work again so soon, but with the hearing less than a week away, Sadie didn't have a moment to waste.

Two hours later, Sadie walked into the recreation department for the town of Breckenridge. She'd stopped at Carter Park and Pavilion first, but the manager there had directed her to the recreation department, stating that they were in charge of ads and promotion.

Sadie impatiently tapped the gray Formica countertop, waiting for someone to appear. After what seemed an eternity, a stocky middle-aged man wearing a yellow shirt that gaped at the buttonholes appeared from a back room. He looked surprised to see Sadie standing there.

"I didn't realize anyone was here," he said, quickly approaching the counter. "May I help you?"

"I hope so." Sadie handed him the pamphlet, already opened to the center page with the photo of Giselle. "That tall girl on the right. Do you know her name?"

Creases appeared on his pale forehead. "Should I know her?"

"Well, I was told this department was in charge of promotions," Sadie explained. "And since this pamphlet was made two months ago according to the date on the back cover, I assume someone here was in charge of hiring the models for these photographs."

His eyes widened. "Oh, you want Charlene. She knows all about this stuff." He held up one finger. "Just wait here, ma'am. I think she's in the back somewhere."

"Thank you," Sadie said, praying that Charlene would recognize the girl.

A short time later, a young African American woman walked through the back entryway and approached Sadie with a smile. She wore a black pantsuit with a pretty gray and yellow scarf. Her dark hair was pulled back into a sleek ponytail, and she looked like she could be a model herself.

"Hello," the woman said to Sadie. "I'm Charlene. Bob told me you want the name of one of the models in our pamphlet."

"Yes," Sadie said, pointing Giselle out to her. "This girl. Do you know her?"

"I sure do. Her name is Carlita Marzan."

Sadie breathed a prayer of thanks. She had a name! Now she just needed some way to contact her. "Do you happen to have her phone number or the name of her modeling agency?"

Charlene laughed. "Modeling agency? Carlita doesn't have an agency. She's my sister's roommate." She reached for a notepad and jotted down a phone number. "But she wants to be a model, so if you're looking for one, just give her a call."

Sadie resisted the urge to leap over the counter and hug Charlene. "Thank you so much. I'll do that."

By the time she reached the parking lot, Sadie had her cell phone out, ready to dial the number Charlene had given her. Then she hesitated. The last thing she wanted to do was scare away Carlita before she got the information she wanted.

Sadie climbed into the Tahoe and thought long and hard about what she should say. Then she took a deep breath and dialed Carlita's number.

The phone picked up on the third ring. "Hello?"

Sadie's heart skipped a beat at the familiar voice. It was definitely the same young woman who had purchased the Steiff teddy bear at the Antique Mine.

Breathe, Sadie reminded herself.

"Hello," Sadie said at last. "Laura Finch." She didn't exactly say *she* was Laura Finch, making her feel slightly better about the fib. She'd decided to use her cousin's name instead of her own. That way if Carlita searched for her online, she'd see that Laura was involved with marketing and promotion. "I saw your modeling work in the Carter Park and Pavilion pamphlet," Sadie told her, "and I was very impressed."

"Thank you," Carlita said. "Are you an agent?"

"No, I'm not," Sadie said, wincing a little at the raw eagerness in the woman's voice. "But I would like to meet with you regarding your work. Do you have any time available today?"

"Well, I'm just leaving for work," Carlita said. "But I'm free tomorrow morning if that works for you. Say around eleven o'clock?"

"Yes, that will work for me," Sadie said. "Where would you like to meet?"

"There's a place called the Bistro on Adams Road. It's quiet, so it's a good place for business meetings."

Sadie wished Carlita had time to meet her today, but she'd just have to be patient. Besides, this would give her time to figure out exactly how to approach Carlita and keep her from bolting once she realized that Laura Finch was really Sadie Speers from the Antique Mine.

"That sounds great," Sadie told her. "See you there."

Maybe tomorrow, Sadie would finally discover who had been trying to frame her.

17

Sadie arrived back in Silver Peak shortly after three o'clock. She headed to the Antique Mine to relieve Julie, who had to pick up her twin boys after school. Then she called her cousin, Laura, and asked if she had time for a chat.

A short time later, Laura appeared in the Antique Mine. She rented the third-floor apartment from Sadie, located in the same building, so she didn't have far to walk for their chat.

"Are you all right?" Laura asked, walking into the empty shop. "It sounded urgent on the phone."

"I'm fine," Sadie said, setting a plate of chocolate chip cookies that she'd just purchased from Arbuckle's between them. "Have a cookie?"

"Uh-oh," Laura said with a knowing smile as she reached for a cookie. "This seems like a bribe."

"Consider it a preemptive thank-you gift."

Laura arched a brow. "Well, that sounds intriguing. What will I do to deserve it?"

Sadie smiled. "You'll let me impersonate you tomorrow for about an hour or so."

"I will?"

Sadie leaned forward on the counter, hoping to make Laura understand. "I'm afraid I already did impersonate you on the telephone." Then she told her about finding Carlita, aka Giselle, and arranging a meeting with her tomorrow morning using Laura's name. "I was afraid if she heard my name she wouldn't even show up and I really need to talk to her."

Concern flashed in Laura's eyes. "Are you sure you'll be safe? It sounds like this woman could be a criminal. Maybe you should turn her in to the police."

"I thought about it," Sadie mused. In truth, it had consumed her thoughts during the drive home from Breckenridge. But she feared Carlita really would clam up if she got the police involved, and then it would be just Sadie's word against Carlita's. "But I think this way is the best. I just hope you don't mind too much."

"You know I'll do anything to help you," Laura told her. "You're welcome to use my name or anything else you need."

Sadie walked around the counter to give her a cousin a hug. "Thank you. It means so much that you're in my corner."

"Always," Laura said with a smile.

Sadie reached for a cookie. "It's possible Carlita may look you up online and try to contact you. I did indicate you might be looking for models. In fact, that's the reason I gave for our meeting."

"What a coincidence," Laura said with a chuckle. "I have a colleague back in Boston who just put a call out for models, but he doesn't want to pay big city prices for one. Too bad this Carlita woman may be in jail soon, or I probably could give her some work."

"She is a knockout," Sadie told her. "And I'm not convinced she's a criminal. She certainly didn't give off that vibe when she came into the Antique Mine. I think it's more likely that someone sent her there to buy the bear."

"But you don't know who?"

"Not yet," Sadie replied. "Or why they'd pay so much money when they intended to give the coin—and the bear—back to me. And I'm running out of time to find out. My hearing is next Monday."

Laura nodded. "I know. I met up with Edwin the other day to discuss this proposed Victorian restoration project. He asked me to be a character witness for you, if it went to trial."

A cold wave washed over Sadie. Just hearing the words made it seem all too real. Could she really go to trial for a crime she didn't commit? Could she possibly be convicted? She took a deep breath, determined not to let the fear of the unknown overwhelm her. "Let's hope it won't come to that."

Laura reached out to give Sadie's arm an encouraging squeeze. "I'm sure it won't. In fact, I'm praying about it every day."

"Thank you," Sadie replied, her throat tight with emotion. Then she took a bite of the cookie, ready to lighten the mood. "But just in case, I'd better fatten up. I doubt jail food is as good as Arbuckle's."

Laura chuckled as she reached for a second cookie. "Then we'd better fill up while we can."

Sadie and Laura ate cookies and chatted until it was time to close the Antique Mine and head home. She only had two more nights left with Sara, and she wanted to enjoy every moment of them.

When Sadie walked into the house a short time later, she inhaled the savory aroma of meat loaf. "Sara?"

"I'm in the kitchen, Grandma."

Sadie set down her purse and slipped out of her jacket before making her way to the kitchen. When she stepped inside, she was surprised to see the table already set. "What's all this?"

"I wanted to make supper for you," Sara told her, setting a bowl of salad on the table. "It's nothing too fancy, just meat loaf and salad and green beans. I used ingredients you already had on hand."

"Good thinking." Sadie had planned to skip supper after indulging in so many chocolate chip cookies, but she wasn't about to spoil Sara's surprise. "This all looks wonderful."

"Go ahead and sit down," Sara told her, walking over to the oven and carefully removing the pan of meat loaf. Hank sat near the refrigerator and watched Sara's every move, ready to scoop up any food that happened to hit the floor.

Sara carried the meat loaf to the table and set the dish on a cast-iron trivet before taking a seat. Then they said grace before digging in.

Despite her full stomach, Sadie enjoyed every bite of Sara's delicious meal. Even more, she relished the easy chatter that flowed between them as Sara told Sadie all about her day at school. After the incident with the lie and catching Sara with Tre at Alice's house, Sadie had feared there might be some remaining tension between them. But the surprise meal and their conversation proved otherwise.

"So, Grandma, can I ask you a question?" Sara forked up a green bean and examined it for a moment before placing it in her mouth.

Sadie sensed a change in the girl's tone. "Of course. You can talk to me about anything."

"I heard some kids at school saying you might go to jail." Sara put down her fork. "Is that true?"

Sadie dabbed at her mouth with her napkin, taken aback by the abrupt change of subject. She wondered if Sara had been worrying about this but afraid to say anything.

"Well, here is what's happening," Sadie began. "There is an evidentiary hearing scheduled this coming Monday. That's when the prosecutor will try to say that he has enough evidence against me for there to be a trial. Edwin will tell my side of the story, and then the judge will decide whether to dismiss the case or go forward with a trial."

Sara's eyes widened with apprehension. "So there could be a trial?"

"It's possible," Sadie said gently. "But we're not there yet, and Edwin is an excellent lawyer. I don't want you to be worried about it."

Sara looked at her. "But aren't you worried, Grandma? I'd be really scared."

Sadie hesitated for a long moment, wanting to find the right words. "I'm frustrated, because I know I didn't steal the coin but I haven't found a way to prove it yet. Sometimes I am scared that no one will believe me and that I won't be able to control what happens." She paused a moment, watching Hank lick up a morsel of meat loaf that had fallen on the floor. "But the truth is that we can't control everything that happens in our lives. That's why we trust God to see us through the tough times."

"But it's not fair," Sara said softly. "You didn't do anything wrong."

"I know." Sadie reached over to squeeze Sara's hand. "But I believe everything happens for a reason. Sometimes we find out why, and sometimes we just have to hold on for the ride."

Sara nodded, although she didn't look convinced. "I guess so."

"And the most important thing," Sadie told her, repeating the words her own grandmother had said to her years ago, "is not to worry about something that might happen in the future, but to enjoy the gift of today that God has given us."

Sara smiled. "So that means we should probably have dessert."

Sadie laughed. "I like the way you think, young lady."

The doorbell rang as Sara walked over and opened the freezer.

Sadie looked over at Sara. "Are you expecting someone?"

"No." Sara pulled out a carton of vanilla ice cream. "Are you?"

"No, I'm not," Sadie said, as the doorbell rang a second time. She walked into the living room, Hank at her heels, and opened the front door. Alice and Theo stood on the other side.

"We're home!" they chorused together.

Sadie let out a cry of delight and then enveloped both of them in a big hug. "What a nice surprise! I had no idea you were coming back tonight."

"We were able to catch an earlier flight," Alice said, "so we decided to head home."

A squeal sounded behind them. "Mom!" Sara shouted. "Theo!" Then she ran toward the door, flying into Alice's arms. "I can't believe you're here!"

Alice gave her daughter a warm squeeze. "How's my girl?"

"I'm good." She stepped back, a wide smile on her face. "I just made supper for Grandma and we're about to have sundaes for dessert."

"I think there's enough for all four of us," Sadie announced. "Do you have time for ice cream or are you ready to get home?"

"That's a silly question," Theo teased, walking into the house. "There's always time for ice cream."

The next day, Sadie arrived at the Bistro in Breckenridge shortly before eleven o'clock. All the tables were empty except one in the far corner that was occupied by two men in business suits, each with a laptop open in front of them.

The restaurant was the type where the customer placed an order at the counter and then carried the food to a table. Sadie ordered an iced tea and then found a table that would give her and Carlita the privacy she wanted.

A moment later, Carlita walked into the shop, dressed for success. She wore a dark blue suit jacket and matching skirt, along with a crisp white blouse and a pair of silver gray spiked heels that made Sadie's own feet hurt just to look at them.

Carlita's gaze landed on Sadie, and a puzzled look crossed her gorgeous face. "You're the lady from that antique store in Silver Peak."

"That's right," Sadie said with a smile, wanting to set her at ease. "I'm here to meet with you."

Carlita placed the black case she carried on top of the table. "But your name isn't Laura Finch."

"And your name isn't Giselle Fleur," Sadie said gently.

That made the woman smile. "Fair enough."

"I do know Laura Finch," Sadie told her. "In fact, I talked to her about you yesterday. She knows about our meeting and your interest in modeling."

Carlita sat down at the table. "I looked her up. According to her Web site, she's involved in a lot of marketing projects that could probably use models."

Sadie nodded toward the briefcase on the table. "What do you have there?"

"My portfolio." Carlita unzipped the briefcase and pulled out a monthly planner, setting it aside to reach into the case once more and retrieve her portfolio.

"May I take a look?" Sadie asked her. The point of this meeting was to gain Carlita's trust. Once she did that, maybe the young woman would answer some of her questions. As a last resort, she could threaten Carlita with a visit from the police, but she didn't want to go there unless absolutely necessary.

"Sure," Carlita said with a dazzling smile. She pushed her portfolio across the table and then rose to her feet. "I'm going to grab a diet soda. Can I get you something?"

"No, thanks," Sadie replied, opening the portfolio. "I'm good."

After Carlita left the table, Sadie started looking at her portfolio. It was full of both candid and professional shots, all of them impressive. Carlita was very photogenic and looked good in everything from a string bikini to a hooded parka. There were a few modeling shots included, such as the Carter Park and Pavilion photographs, and all of them were local.

Sadie glanced at the front counter and saw Carlita engaged in conversation with one of the businessmen from the other table. Turning her attention back to the portfolio, Sadie flipped a page and saw Carlita standing on a makeshift fashion runway, modeling a retro, black circle skirt and leopard-skin top. Then she recognized another familiar face. May Cooley, Val's roommate, stood off to one side, watching with a notebook in one hand and a pen in the other.

"That nice guy bought my diet soda for me," Carlita said, resuming her seat. "He asked for my phone number too, but he's too old for me. I think he's almost thirty."

Sadie smiled to herself, assuming that Carlita was experienced in fending off interested males. "Is this May?" she asked, pointing to Val's roommate in the photo.

Carlita glanced at it, stirring her soda with a straw. "Yes, that's at her fashion show last spring. It was a lot of fun."

"Was the show some kind of class project?"

"No, May's trying to sell some of her designs before she graduates. Her brother buys a lot of her fabric and sewing equipment with the money he makes mowing lawns at fancy houses in Breckenridge. He calls himself an investor."

Sadie looked at Carlita. "Fancy houses, like the mansion owned by Brent Fielder?"

"Probably." Carlita frowned. "Are you here to talk about a modeling job or about May?"

Sadie didn't want Carlita to leave yet, especially now that she'd found a connection between Carlita and the Steiff teddy bear. A connection that ran through Val and May. "I know Laura is interested in your doing some modeling. What does your schedule look like?"

Carlita took a sip of her soda and then opened her weekly planner. "I've got quite a few openings for modeling assignments if you have any jobs in mind." She flipped to the current month, where some of the days were already filled in.

Even reading upside down, Sadie could see the name *May Cooley* penciled in on the day before Carlita came to the Antique Mine to buy the teddy bear. She leaned forward, just to be sure she wasn't mistaken. But May's name was there in black and white.

"Is May planning to have you model in another fashion show soon?" Sadie asked, trying to stay calm as the pieces started to come together. "I see you had her penciled in earlier this month."

Carlita glanced down at the planner. "Oh yeah, we did meet, but it wasn't about a fashion show. She won't have another one of those until the spring. They're so much fun though! She has such great accessories—all kinds of purses, shoes, jewelry, and wigs. A girl can go crazy dressing up in her stuff."

"Wigs?" Sadie said, thinking of the blonde woman Spike had seen tossing something over the back fence of the Antique Mine. Could that have been May wearing a blonde wig?

"Yes, in all different colors, including purple and orange. It's fun."

Sadie knew that the meeting May had with Carlita had to be more than a coincidence, but she wanted to find out for certain. "May must have really liked your work since she hired you to go to the Antique Mine and buy that teddy bear."

"I suppose she did," Carlita said warily, her gaze on Sadie. "Did I pull it off, do you think? May was really worried that I'd overdo it."

"You did pull it off," Sadie said, stunned that she'd already met May, the person who had set this whole thing in motion. Perhaps Val had been in on it too, Sadie thought to herself.

"And leaving the coin inside the teddy bear was genius," Sadie told Carlita, carefully watching her expression.

Confusion filled her brown eyes. "What coin?"

"The one inside the teddy bear."

Carlita's delicate nose wrinkled. "Why would anyone put a coin inside a teddy bear?"

Her reaction made it clear that Carlita was clueless about the Huntley counterfeit coin. Which meant that May had used her as a dupe.

Suddenly, Sadie felt bad for meeting Carlita here under false pretenses. The portfolio and the girl's eagerness made it clear how important a modeling career was to her. It wasn't Carlita's fault that she'd been unknowingly involved in a crime.

"You know, I think Laura will be very impressed with you." Sadie reached into her purse and drew out a piece of paper. "I'm going to give you her e-mail address, and I want you to contact her about some possible modeling jobs. And I'll let her know that you'll be in touch."

"Really?" Carlita exclaimed, taking the paper Sadie handed to her and pressing it to her heart. "You don't know how much this means to me. How can I ever thank you?"

Sadie smiled, finally seeing a path to clear her name. "You already did."

18

SADIE WALKED TO ALFRED'S OFFICE, EAGER TO TALK TO HIM about what she'd just learned from Carlita. She still didn't have all the pieces of the puzzle, but she sensed that she was close to figuring them out.

When Sadie arrived at his open office door, she saw Val in there alone seated at a desk, her head bent over a stack of papers and a red pen in one hand.

Sadie hesitated a moment and then tapped lightly on the door.

Val looked up. "Oh, hello, Ms. Speers. I'm afraid Professor Daly already left for the day. He had a meeting to attend in Denver."

"That's all right," Sadie said, walking into the office. "That gives me a chance to talk to you."

Interest sparked in Val's eyes. She set down her pen. "What about?"

"Your roommate."

Val blinked. "May?"

Sadie took a seat in the empty chair that Alfred kept near his desk. "Yes. Actually, Val, I think she may be involved in a crime."

Val laughed. "You're joking."

Sadie didn't say anything, watching as Val's laughter began to fade.

"You're not joking?" Val asked her, frowning now.

"I'm afraid not. What can you tell me about May? Did you know her before you became roommates?"

"No," Val said slowly, "but we've been roommates for the last three years, and you get to know someone pretty well when you're stuck together in a small space."

Sadie glanced at the door, noticing students walking by, but none of them seemed to be able to hear her conversation with Val. Still, she got up and closed the door, wanting the privacy and hoping it would encourage Val to speak freely. "Did you ever leave the teddy bear alone with her?"

"No," Val said, and then she hesitated. "Well, I guess I did when I took a shower that Sunday evening before the auction. She was studying when I left the room."

"How long do you think you were out of the room?"

"Well, I like long showers, so it was probably thirty minutes before I came back. Only the door was locked and I hadn't taken my key with me." Val shook her head at the memory. "There I was, stuck in the hallway, wearing only my bathrobe and a towel wrapped around my head. I must have knocked for a good five minutes before May opened the door."

"Why did it take her so long?"

"May said she'd fallen asleep while she was studying, which does happen a lot, actually. She puts in a lot of long hours to keep her perfect grade point average." Val stood up and began to pace in the small office. Her long gray sweatshirt hung loosely on her shoulders, and she had a small hole in one knee of her blue jeans.

"Do you know Carlita Marzan?" Sadie asked her.

Val stopped and turned toward her. "No, should I?"

"She did some modeling for one of May's fashion shows. Did you go to the one last spring?"

Val shook her head. "I spent last semester studying in Italy, so I missed it. What does this Carlita person have to do with all of this?"

"She's involved in the crime," Sadie told her, though she didn't add that Carlita seemed unaware of her complicity.

Val plopped back down in her chair. "Look, Ms. Speers, I know how much Professor Daly respects you, so I won't say that you're wrong, but you just don't know May like I do. She's as straitlaced as they come. Now, her brother—that's another story."

"Alex?" Sadie said, surprised at the anger she heard in Val's voice.

"Yes. I thought he was so cute and sweet whenever he'd come to our dorm room to visit May. I was impressed that he had his own business and was helping May build her fashion design career. When he asked me out on a date, I was on cloud nine."

"And?" Sadie prompted.

"And it was a disaster. Alex's charm is about a mile wide but only an inch deep. His idea of romance was to have me teach him how to pick locks. At first, it was kind of fun, but he just wouldn't let it go. We were at it for three solid hours before I finally told him I had a migraine and he had to take me home." Val shook her head. "That's when May warned me about him."

Sadie sat up in her chair. "What did she say?

Val sighed. "She told me that she loved her brother, but that he'd had...problems. Apparently, he had to drop out of college because of some cheating scandal. And he'd had some brushes with the law. She'd asked him to help her build her career mainly to keep him busy and out of trouble."

"And did that work?"

Val shrugged. "I don't know. But it made our date seem a lot more ominous. He asked me out shortly after finding out my dad is a locksmith, if that tells you anything."

It told Sadie even more than she'd expected to hear. Alex's lawn business would allow him access to some of the wealthiest neighborhoods—and a chance to walk around those neighborhoods without raising suspicions. He could get to know the people there and gain their trust. Perhaps even find an excuse to go inside some of those houses and see the layout.

"What kind of car does Alex drive?"

"A blue Camry," Val said. "Why?"

"Just wondering," Sadie said, although she'd had a very specific reason for asking. Val's description of Alex's car matched the one that had followed her and Roz for so long on their way back from the Ferris auction.

Suddenly, Val shot up out of her chair. "Wait a minute. Is this why you sent that letter to the post office box? Do you think May did something with that teddy bear? Something…illegal?"

Sadie met her gaze. "May, or her brother, or both. I even thought you might have been involved, but you were so racked with guilt over taking the teddy bear to your dorm room without permission that I knew you wouldn't have planted stolen property inside."

Val went white. "Stolen property? Is that what this is about?"

"Yes, and the Steiff teddy bear is involved. Sometime between the time that Alfred put the teddy bear in your control to the time

I bought it at the auction, someone planted a stolen Huntley silver dollar inside the bear."

Val reached out to grab the chair, looking a little sick now. "Huntley silver dollar?" she gasped. "One stolen from Brent Fielder's collection?"

"Val, are you okay?" Sadie asked, hurrying toward the girl, who looked like she was about to faint. "I think you need to sit down."

Val allowed Sadie to assist her back in the chair. She drew in a few deep breaths until the color returned to her face.

"Since Brent had all ten Huntley counterfeit coins," Sadie said at last, "it had to be one from his collection. It seems May tried to frame me for the crime."

"I didn't know," Val whispered.

Sadie believed her. Val might not have liked Brent Fielder, but she doubted the woman would risk her career by stealing the Huntley coins. And she certainly wouldn't have admitted to Sadie or anyone else that she'd taken the teddy bear to her dorm room if she knew she could be implicated in a crime.

Val sucked in a deep breath. "I started all of this by taking that bear to my room, so I should help fix it." She met Sadie's gaze. "What can I do?"

Sadie thought about it for a long moment. "You can tell me where May is right now."

The door to the dorm room stood open, and Sadie could hear classical music playing inside. She stood in the doorway, watching May pin a piece of muslin cloth to the dressmaker's dummy in the corner. May's back was to her, so the young woman had no idea that Sadie was watching her.

Sadie tapped on the door.

May turned around, one hand on her chest. "Oh, you startled me."

"I'm sorry," Sadie told her. "Can I come in?"

May hesitated. "Val isn't here."

"I know," Sadie told her, stepping inside the room. "I want to talk to you before I go to the police."

Her brow wrinkled. "I don't understand."

"The thread you used on the Steiff teddy bear didn't quite match the original thread," Sadie said evenly. "However, I'm sure the police can find the spool of thread you used to sew up the seam after you placed the stolen Huntley coin inside."

May held up both hands. "Wait...just wait a minute." Panic flashed in her green eyes. "I need time to think."

"I met with Carlita at the Bistro this morning," Sadie said, knowing now was the time to push, when May was caught off guard. Sadie needed the truth, and she couldn't wait for it any longer. "Carlita told me everything, including how you met with her and instructed her to come to the Antique Mine and buy the Steiff teddy bear. You knew the Huntley silver dollar was inside. That's why you wanted it back."

"No," May said, her voice almost a whisper.

"What I can't figure out," Sadie said, taking another step closer to her, "is why you gave me back the teddy bear with the coin still inside it. And why steal the coin from Brent Fielder in the first place? Was it to fund your fashion design line? Or to pay back your brother for everything he's done for you?"

May took a step back and closed her eyes. "Everything he's done for me?" She opened her eyes again, anger blazing in them.

"You don't understand! All he's done is made a mess of his life. A mess that I keep having to clean up. But I won't go to jail for him. Not after I've tried so hard to keep him out of trouble."

The final piece of the puzzle clicked in Sadie's mind. "You weren't trying to frame me for stealing the Huntley coin. You were trying to protect me from your brother. That's why you hired Carlita to buy back the teddy bear. So I wouldn't have it when your brother called in the anonymous tip to the police."

"That's right." May walked over to the window and stared outside. "I found out that Alex was responsible for the recent thefts in Breckenridge. I begged him to stop, but he told me the police already suspected him. His plan was to turn their suspicion to someone else and he needed my help."

May turned around to face Sadie. "We lost our parents when were were twelve years old. Alex didn't handle it well...and I've been taking care of him ever since." She shook her head. "I must have done something wrong, because he's always trying to cut corners to get what he wants."

"Whose idea was it to put the Huntley coin in the teddy bear?"

"Alex's," May said, her voice flat. "Val had showed him the teddy bear and told him it was going to be up for sale at the Ferris estate auction if he was interested. She actually believes he earns a lot of money with his lawn business."

"So he put the coin inside the teddy bear on Sunday evening," Sadie ventured, "while Val was in the shower?"

May nodded. "I caught him doing it. That's when he explained his plan. He'd go to the Ferris auction and watch to see who won the teddy bear. Then he'd plant a GPS tracking device on their car or somewhere, so he could track it and discover their identity.

After that, all he had to do was call in a tip to the police, who would find the stolen coin inside the teddy bear—with no way to connect it to Alex."

Sadie tilted her head to one side, wondering if she could believe her. "How do I know what you're saying is true?"

"Because I spent twenty-four hundred dollars of my student loan money to buy the teddy bear back," May exclaimed. "And that's not including the money I paid Giselle to get it."

Sadie took a step toward her. "But you didn't remove the coin."

May's face fell. "Yes, I did. And then I brought the teddy bear back to you and tossed it over the fence. Only I didn't know…"

The truth suddenly dawned on Sadie. "You didn't know that Alex had put *two* of the Huntley coins he'd stolen into the teddy bear?"

She gave a slow nod. "I'm so sorry. Will you let me fix this?"

"How?" Sadie asked, wondering if she could trust the girl.

May squared her shoulders. "I'll show you."

An hour later, Sadie sat in the campus coffee shop, gently stirring a tall mocha latte in front of her.

"Here he comes," May said from the next table. She didn't look at Sadie as she spoke, her gaze focused on her brother.

Alex didn't recognize Sadie as he sat down at the table next to May. Sadie reached up to adjust the long black wig that May had dressed her in, along with a pair of horn-rimmed glasses and a baggy gray Colorado Mountain College sweatshirt. Sadie had barely recognized herself after May had finished applying makeup to her face and added some jewelry to finish the disguise.

Now, as she sat right next to May and Alex's table, she could hear every word they were saying.

"What is the big emergency?" Alex asked his sister. "I have work to do."

"It's over," May said, the pain evident in her voice. "I've tried to protect you for so long, Alex, but I just can't do it anymore."

Alex leaned toward her. "Lower your voice. Nothing is over. It's just beginning. I've got a buyer for the coins. As soon as the sale goes through, I'll have the seed money I need to expand my lawn business."

"So you can steal even more from your customers?" May shook her head. "This has got to stop. You've got to confess."

Sadie heard the sound of Alex's chair scraping the tile floor as he moved closer to his sister. "No, you've got to quit getting in my way. Your interference with that stupid teddy bear almost ruined my plan. Fortunately, you gave it back to her not realizing there was still another coin inside, so the heat is off of me." He shook his head. "Your guilty conscience is your Achilles' heel, May. The sooner you get rid of it, the better off we'll both be."

"It's too late," May told him. "The police have already been called. and they're on their way."

He leaned back in his chair, folding his arms across his chest. "You're bluffing."

"Alex, listen to me," May implored, placing a hand on his arm. "You've got to come clean now. Maybe they'll give you a break if you confess, turn in the coins and all the other stuff you stole, and try to make restitution."

"Or," he posited, shaking off her hand, "I could tell them this was all *your* plan from the beginning. After all, you're the one who sewed the coins into the teddy bear."

"Only because I had a plan to stop you," May replied. "I never should have done it in the first place, but I was trying to make it right. I didn't know you put a second coin in the bear."

"Nobody will believe that," Alex told her. "Certainly not the police. So if you don't want to spend the next several years designing prison garb, you'd better call the police back and tell them you made a mistake."

"I told you," May said, her voice tight with tears, "they're on their way."

Alex smirked. "And I still say you're bluffing."

"No, she's not, Alex." Sadie stood up and took off her wig, causing some of the students around her to gasp. "The police are on their way because I'm the one who called them."

As if on cue, a siren sounded in the distance.

Alex stared at Sadie in disbelief, then at his sister. "What is this, some kind of trap?"

"No," Sadie told him. "It's two people trying to do the right thing."

"Well, I'm outta here," Alex said, bolting for the door.

Several students blocked his path to the door, leaving him with no way out. He looked at his sister. "May, how could you do this to me?"

"Don't you get it, Alex?" May said, tears flooding her eyes. "I can't protect you from yourself anymore. You have to face the consequences, or it's only going to get worse—for both of us."

Alex turned away from her as two police officers walked through the door. May turned to Sadie, a look of anguish on her face. "Why does doing the right thing have to be so hard?"

"I don't know, May," Sadie said, placing a hand on the girl's shoulder. "But you'll get through this. And Alex will be better for it, if he chooses to be."

Sadie turned to watch the police take Alex out of the coffee shop. She still needed to stop by the police station and give them her statement, as well as call Edwin and Alice and tell them the news.

But for now, she just thanked God for showing her the way to the truth.

That evening, Sadie snuggled under the thick quilts on her bed and read Nora Primm's diary. The hour was growing late, but she was still too alert to sleep after the long, eventful day.

She'd made her statement to the Breckenridge police, along with May and Carlita. The Breckenridge police had then sent their report to Sheriff Mac Slattery. According to Edwin, a formal request had been made to drop the charges against her.

Sadie breathed a sigh of relief, feeling lighter than she had in days. The shadow that had been hanging over her was finally gone, and she could celebrate her birthday on Saturday with a full and happy heart.

A wolf howled in the distance and she could hear the wind rattling the branches outside her window. She settled into her pillow, relishing the warmth of her bed, and wiggled her toes under the blankets.

Then she turned the page of the diary, realizing she was close to finishing it. The long courtship of Nora and E. had remained a secret throughout the winter and spring of 1904, but Sadie sensed that was about to change.

June 5, 1904

Silver Peak, Colorado

Dear Diary,

Oh, joyful day!

E. has been hired as an apprentice by one of the finest silver-smiths in town. He's dabbled in the craft for a while, but now he can hone his skills and prove himself worthy of me. It's been a long time coming, but I know our plan will come to fruition. Patience is the key. I practice it daily ever since Mother has taken it upon herself to learn how to play the piano. Sometimes I think she plays it just to drive Father out of the house.

But no matter.

Soon, dearest Ethan will fulfill my dreams and it will be the sweetest victory of my life.

Sadie sat up in bed, staring at the page in front of her. "Ethan?" she said out loud. "Who is Ethan?"

She'd assumed this whole time that the man Nora referred to as *E.* in her diary had been Eustace. Was it possible that Nora had been pining for a man named Ethan instead?

Turning back to the diary, she began flipping through the pages, looking for answers. And what she found made her look at the tragic love story of Nora Primm and Eustace Huntley in a whole new light.

19

————

"WELL, THIS IS A NICE SURPRISE," BRENT FIELDER SAID, ENTERING the Victorian room where Sadie waited for him. It was the same room she'd been placed in before, and she'd been biding her time there for the last twenty minutes.

But her reason for coming here was too important to let the wait bother her. "I heard that all ten of the Huntley counterfeit coins were returned to you."

"Yes, they were. Thank you so much, Sadie, for your part in catching the thief."

"You're welcome."

He flashed a smile. "I had to give the insurance money back, but I got some nice publicity from it that brought some new potential buyers my way, so it all worked out in the end."

"I'm glad to hear it."

"So"—he took a seat in the chair next to her—"what brings you here, Sadie?"

She held up the Nora Primm diary. "Have you ever read this?"

His brow furrowed. "Well…no. I just haven't found the time. Besides, I'm not much of a reader."

"I found it quite enlightening."

"Really?" He arched a brow. "How so?"

"Well, as you might have guessed, Nora does write about Eustace Huntley in her diary."

"Of course she does," Brent said. "He was the love of her life and she was devoted to him until the end."

"May I ask where exactly you found her diary? I only wonder because it's surprising to me that its contents haven't been revealed before."

"Actually, it was quite a lucky find," Brent told her. "Another collector, one much like myself, passed away at his home in Denver, and all the contents of the house were put up for auction. He had a large collection of diaries and journals that spanned a couple of centuries. When I learned that a diary by Nora Primm was among them, I recognized the name from the Huntley story and had to have her diary to go along with my collection of Huntley coins."

"I see," Sadie said, wondering how best to break the news to him. "Actually, the Huntley story is flawed."

His brow furrowed. "What do you mean?"

Sadie settled into her chair. "Well, to begin with, Nora Primm and Eustace Huntley had a complicated relationship. You see, they did fall in love and plan to marry. But Eustace didn't think he was good enough for her and broke off their engagement."

Brent chuckled. "I'm sorry, but you're wrong. They were engaged when Eustace went to prison. It was printed in all the newspapers at the time. I can show you the articles if you'd like."

"Oh, I believe you," Sadie said with a smile. "But, you see, that was their *second* engagement. Nora actually referred to it that way in her diary. In fact, I believe she wrote about her first broken engagement quite vehemently, but later tore those pages out of her diary." She handed the diary to him. "If you look inside, you can see where some pages have been ripped from the spine."

Brent pulled the diary from the plastic bag and opened it.

"The yellowing of the paper," Sadie explained, "and the fraying of the ripped paper edges shows that the pages were torn out decades ago, most likely by Nora herself, although I suppose a family member might have done it."

"But why rip them out?" Brent asked, a gleam of curiosity in his eye.

"Because they probably detailed her scheme to get revenge on the man who had dumped her." Sadie folded her hands in her lap. "When I first started reading the diary, I was struck by how devoted Nora seemed to be to the man she referred to as E. She wrote of secret meetings with him and how she needed to be patient. In fact, she kept repeating the phrase *patience is the key.*"

"Hardly surprising," Brent countered with a confident smile. "They say patience is a virtue."

"What I discovered as I kept reading," Sadie continued, "was that Nora wasn't waiting to wed the man she loved—the man she kept referring to as E. in her diary. She was waiting to wreak her revenge on Eustace for breaking their first engagement."

Brent held both hands up in the air. "Wait a minute. Isn't Eustace the man she refers to as E.?"

Sade smiled. "I thought so too, until she called him Ethan in one of the entries. I'm not sure if that was an oversight or by design, but it made me do some more digging into Eustace Huntley's story. It seems that he took on an apprentice in the summer of 1904 named Ethan Fonner. Six months later, Eustace was arrested for using counterfeit silver dollars. The *D-for-Denver* mint designation on the coins finally did him in, since Denver didn't mint 1904 coins. Rather a sloppy mistake for a meticulous craftsman, don't you think?"

"I suppose," Brent said slowly. "But I'm still not getting the connection."

"That's because you haven't read the diary," Sadie said kindly. "You see, in the diary, Nora slowly lays out her plan to woo Ethan until he falls in love with her. So much in love that he'd do anything she asked of him. He was a simple farm boy, and she was a rich girl from town. He really didn't stand a chance."

His eyes gleamed with curiosity. "And what did she ask of Ethan?"

Sadie leaned forward in her chair. "She asked him to forge ten counterfeit Morgan silver dollars. And to place them in the pockets of Eustace's pants, where he routinely carried his silver dollars. And to do something to the coins to make Eustace get caught."

Brent stared at her. "You can't be serious!"

"It's all in there," she said, pointing to Nora's diary. "Ethan Fonner made those counterfeit coins at the behest of Nora Primm. When Ethan finally realized that Nora didn't love him and had just been using him to hurt Eustace, he fled Colorado, never to return. And Nora hurried to her ex-fiancé's side, vowing that she believed in his innocence and would stand beside him through it all."

"Wow," Brent exclaimed. "Did that really happen?"

"It did," Sadie said evenly. "And, of course, Nora was telling the truth—Eustace *was* innocent—but she was the only one in town who knew that for a fact." She sighed. "Her loyalty to Eustace made him fall in love with her all over again and they were once again engaged to be married. But he died shortly after his release from prison, never knowing his fiancée had betrayed him so ruthlessly."

Brent looked both mesmerized and horrified by the story. "Do you think she actually would have married him after what she did?"

"I don't know," Sadie answered honestly. "Nora set out to destroy him and succeeded beyond her wildest dreams. The diary ends during the first year of his incarceration, and she writes mainly about mundane household affairs at that point, never referring to Eustace—or Ethan—again."

A deep flush stained both of his cheeks. "That's absolutely diabolical. And it makes a great story! When the diary goes public, it will probably double the value of the coins!"

Sadie couldn't help but smile at the man's enthusiasm. And it *was* a compelling story, she had to admit, although a deeply tragic one. She just wished the truth had been discovered during Eustace's lifetime.

On Saturday afternoon, Sadie began to prepare for her birthday dinner at the Putnams' house. Edwin was due to pick her up at six o'clock, and despite Roz's insistence that Sadie not bring anything, she'd whipped together an apple pie, Roscoe's favorite, and placed it in a plastic pie tote to take tonight.

Then Sadie started getting herself ready for the dinner, which took more time than the pie. Sadie was just putting the finishing touches on her makeup when her cell phone rang.

She looked down to see Alice's name on the screen and then quickly wiped the rose blush off her fingertips before picking up the phone. "Hello, dear."

"Hi, Mom. Are you busy?"

"I'm just getting ready for my birthday dinner tonight."

"Oh, that's right," Alice said, her sigh carrying over the phone. "I forgot about that. And happy birthday, by the way!"

"Thank you." There was something in Alice's tone that didn't sound right to Sadie. "Are you okay?"

"I'm fine," Alice replied. "The kids are fine. Well, Theo is fine. Sara, on the other hand…" Another sigh. "Oh, Mom, I just don't know what to do with that girl."

"What happened?"

"I don't want to talk about it over the phone," Alice said, "and certainly not on your birthday. It can wait."

"Nonsense," Sadie told her. "I'm ready to go and have plenty of time before Edwin will be here to pick me up for dinner. I'm coming over."

"Mom, really, you don't have to."

"See you in a few minutes." Sadie hung up the phone, eager to see Alice and the kids, but a little worried at the same time.

What had Sara done now?

Sadie drove into Silver Peak, relishing the beauty of the glorious fall day. She waved to Spike, who strode along the sidewalk in front of the Market, and then turned onto the street that would lead her to Alice's house.

She pulled up along the curb to park the Tahoe, remembering the last time when Tre's pickup truck had been there. Something told her that Tre was probably involved in today's dustup too.

Sadie walked to the door and knocked.

"Come in," Alice called out to her.

Sadie walked inside, ready to calm her daughter and try to talk some sense into her granddaughter. Instead she found herself surrounded by a roomful of people.

"Surprise!" they all shouted.

Familiar faces filled every crook and crevice of Alice's large living room and they were all smiling at her.

"What's going on?" Sadie asked, her heart racing in her chest.

Alice laughed as she came forward to hug Sadie. "Mom, this is your surprise birthday party!"

Now it was Sadie's turn to laugh, along with the rest of the guests. "Wow, you are a great actress," she told Alice. "You had me believing something was really wrong."

Alice smiled and performed a curtsy.

Sadie looked around the room and saw Edwin front and center, with Roz and Roscoe standing beside him. The Sweetings were there, along with Claribel, Doc Conroy, and all the Hendersons. Laura stood next to Alfred and Cecile, and Julie and her husband, Chad, waved to her from a back corner of the living room. There were too many people for her to count, and each one had come to celebrate with her.

"Oh, this is wonderful!" Sadie exclaimed at last, clapping her hands together. "Thank you all so much!"

"It's our pleasure," Harry Polmiller called out. Sadie had given Harry his silver platter yesterday and told him about Eustace Huntley. He'd gotten choked up when he'd seen the platter restored to its original beauty.

"Now, where's the cake?" Harry shouted.

Harry's question provoked more laughter as the crowd broke into small groups and began to mingle with one another.

Theo came up to Sadie and gave her a hug. "Happy birthday, Grandma! Were you really surprised?"

Sadie chuckled. "If you could feel the way my heart is pounding right now, you'd know the answer without even asking!"

"But it's a healthy pounding, right?" Roz asked, coming up behind Sadie to give her a hug.

"Yes, it's healthy," Sadie said with a smile. "The kind that happens when your best friend has you totally fooled."

Roscoe chuckled beside her. "You should have seen your face when you walked through that door, Sadie. I about busted a gut laughing."

Sadie shook her finger at him. "Well, we'll see who has the last laugh. I made an apple pie to bring to dinner at your place tonight, Roscoe. Now it's going to stay in my kitchen."

Roz playfully swatted Sadie's arm. "You weren't supposed to bring anything to your birthday dinner!"

"You mean my make-believe birthday dinner?" Sadie said, laughing at Roz's reaction. "You can't be mad if there was never a dinner in the first place."

"Apple pie, huh?" Roscoe said thoughtfully. "That's my favorite." Then he grinned. "We'll be over tomorrow after church to help you eat it."

"Sounds good to me," Sadie told him.

Laura approached her with a hug. "You look beautiful! Almost as if you knew you were coming to a party."

"Well, I'm just glad I didn't wear my dirty garden shoes and one of T.R.'s old shirts."

Laura giggled. "Speaking of beautiful, I met with Carlita and she'll be perfect for the ad campaign my colleague is planning. She leaves for Boston next week."

"How wonderful!" Sadie exclaimed, truly happy for the aspiring model. She and Laura chatted for a while before Sadie made the rounds to mingle with the other guests.

She found Alfred and Cecile each sipping a cupful of fruit punch. "Well, this is a nice surprise," Sadie told them. "Thank you so much for coming."

"We wouldn't miss it," Cecile said, giving Sadie a warm hug. "And we have to tell you our news, since you were so instrumental in making it happen."

"What news?" Sadie asked, looking back and forth between them.

Alfred cleared his throat. "Brent Fielder invited me to his home and presented me with one of the Huntley counterfeit coins in restitution for what happened with my Steiff teddy bear."

Sadie blinked. "Well, that's…unexpected. I didn't realize Brent was so generous."

"Well, Mr. Fielder made sure there was plenty of press there to publicize his generosity," Cecile said with a smile. "And the value of the Huntley coins has been skyrocketing ever since."

"It seems that story you uncovered in Nora Primm's diary really captured the attention of a lot of collectors," Alfred remarked. "And selling that coin Fielder bestowed upon me will recoup the rest of the retirement money I lost in that silly investment."

Cecile reached for her husband's hand. "And we'll have enough money left over for that trip to Paris."

"As well as enough to buy my Steiff bear back," Alfred added, turning to Sadie. "If you're willing to sell it back to me."

"Sold!" Sadie said, so happy for her friends. "But you can give the money to May Cooley. I think she's suffered enough for her part in her brother's mischief."

It took twenty minutes after the party started for Sadie to finally find her way to Edwin. "So," she said to him, "how long have you known about this surprise party?"

His eyes twinkled. "Only a few weeks."

"A few weeks!" she exclaimed. "How did everyone manage to keep it a secret all this time?"

"Well, it wasn't easy, but I had a partner in crime." He waved Sara over to them. "This girl really helped a lot."

Sadie stared at her granddaughter. "You knew about this too!"

"Of course," Sara said with a giggle. "I had to play the bad girl to keep you from suspecting anything."

"Although," Alice said, joining their group, "you played the part a little too well, young lady. You weren't supposed to bring a boy to the house."

"But, Mom! I had to," Sara explained. "I told you on the phone the night that Grandma tattled on me that Tre needed to download pictures from our computer to make Grandma's birthday CD."

"Well, you little stinker," Sadie said, wrapping an arm around Sara's shoulders and giving her an affectionate squeeze. "You really had me worried there for a while."

Sara turned to Alice. "Should we have Grandma open her presents soon?" She pointed to a card table in the corner of the dining room that was piled high with colorful gifts.

"Oh my," Sadie mused, looking at the tall stack through the crowd of people gathered in the dining room, "where am I going to put all that?"

"Oh, Mom!" Alice started laughing. "What a thing to say."

Sadie chuckled. "When you're my age, dear, that's one of the first things that comes to mind."

Edwin cleared his throat. "Speaking of presents, Theo is helping to set up my gift for you, but first..." He reached into his suit pocket and pulled out a small envelope.

"What's this?" Sadie asked as he handed it to her.

"My bill for legal services." A playful twinkle lit his blue eyes. "You'll be glad to know that, as of today, the criminal charge against you has been officially dropped."

Sadie sent up a silent prayer of thanks. "That's the only birthday present I need!"

"Well, it's not the only one you're going to get," Alice told her. "And Edwin says that Alex Cooley agreed to a plea deal with the Breckenridge prosecutor, so you won't have to testify at his trial."

Sadie was glad to hear it, and even more glad for May Cooley, who would have had a very difficult time testifying against her brother. "I've been praying for them both."

"Me too," Edwin said. Then he nodded toward the envelope. "Aren't you curious about your bill?"

"A little," Sadie admitted, slitting the seal with her fingernail. "And I'm really hoping I got the girlfriend discount." Then she looked down at the invoice, which looked exactly like a legal bill.

Only, under the line *Charges for Services Rendered* were the words *One Birthday Dance.*

Sadie grinned as she looked up at Edwin. "I think I can manage to pay that bill. Just let me know where and when."

He looked around the room. "How about here and now?" Then he called out, "Hit it, Theo!"

Sadie mentally braced herself, not sure what to expect next. Then she heard the lilting melody of a familiar song. She turned toward the music, sounding a little scratchy but clear and loud, which emanated from the dining room. The crowd parted to reveal a phonograph against the dining room wall. And not just any phonograph. It was a Victor Orthophonic Credenza model, exactly like the one she'd bid on—and lost—at the Ferris estate auction.

Theo stood next to the phonograph, his gaze on the spinning 78 rpm record.

Her mouth gaped as she turned to Edwin. He smiled at her and held out his hand. "Shall we?"

She accepted his invitation, still speechless, as he took her into his arms and they began to dance to "This Magic Moment."

Sadie took a moment to collect herself, reeling from the thoughtfulness Edwin had put into his gift. She'd had no idea he'd remembered the song from their first dance.

She looked up at his handsome face. "Where did you find that phonograph?"

He smiled. "Do you like it?"

"Like it? I love it. It's exactly like the one I bid on in Breckenridge."

"I know. That's where I got it. I sent an agent there to bid on it in case you didn't win it. I wanted to give you the perfect birthday gift."

Sadie thought back to her bidding war with Herbert Wynot for the phonograph. After the price had gotten too high for Sadie, a new bidder had entered the fray for the Orthophonic. He must have been Edwin's agent.

"After the party," Edwin continued, "we'll take the phonograph to your house and set it up. Unless you'd rather do it tomorrow."

She stared at him, touched beyond belief. "You don't mean the phonograph is mine? Oh, Edwin, it's much too valuable."

"And worth every penny," he said softly. "Happy birthday, my sweet Sadie."

Sadie smiled, silently thanking God for all of her blessings, as she leaned her head against Edwin's broad shoulder and danced with him to the music.

It truly was a magic moment.

About the Author

CAROLE JEFFERSON IS THE PEN NAME FOR A TEAM OF WRITERS who have come together to create the series Mysteries of Silver Peak. *The Counterfeit Caper* was written by Kristin Eckhardt. Kristin is the author of more than forty books, including twenty-one books for Guideposts. She's won two national awards for her writing, and her first book was made into a TV movie. Kristin and her husband have three children and live in central Nebraska. Kristin enjoys quilting, traveling, and spending time with family and friends.

Read on for a sneak peek of another exciting book in Mysteries of Silver Peak!

A Blessing and a Curse

"THE SPECIAL EXHIBIT IS RIGHT THROUGH HERE." SADIE SPEERS looked back to make sure the others were following her before she started across the main gallery of the American Mining Museum. It was easy to get distracted here, and sure enough, she'd already lost a couple of her guests. Sadie had been through this museum dozens of times, and she still always found herself lingering by displays and exhibits she'd never noticed before and getting sucked into rooms she'd been through again and again. This place was… well—Sadie had to laugh—a *goldmine* of information about the history of her hometown Silver Peak.

Sadie couldn't blame Roz, her best friend, for getting distracted by the display of precious metals that had been pulled from the nearby hills. Sadie had spent hours studying the smooth gold nuggets and the flakes of copper and zinc. But Sadie was excited to show her guests the displays she'd been working on, and knew she had to keep them moving.

"We're right behind you Mrs. Speers," Aiden Daly said, ushering his uncle Alfred forward through the room. Aiden was an intern at the museum this summer, brought on to help the small museum with social media, and he had been helping Sadie work on the displays for the Silver Festival whenever he had time. He was as proud of what they'd put together as Sadie was, and now she flashed him a smile, grateful for his help escorting their guests through the museum.

"Hey now. You can't expect someone like me to rush through a history museum," Alfred said, huffing as Aiden pulled him away from a set of photographs of the shantytowns that had sprung up around the earliest mines. Alfred's white hair was getting long in the back, and it brushed the collar of his polo shirt.

"Someone like you?" Roz asked, peeking into a doorway that led to the 3-D model of a silver mine built for children to explore. The museum was housed in an old brick building that had started life as a schoolhouse, and though the first floor was mostly given over to one large gallery room, there were plenty of nooks and crannies to get lost in. "You mean an old geezer?"

Alfred laughed, a deep, good-natured laugh, and he started to move toward the doorway Sadie was ushering them all toward.

"I meant a distinguished professor of history," Alfred said, pretending she had just insulted his dignity. Alfred was a history professor at Colorado Mountain College in nearby Breckenridge, and he specialized in Rocky Mountain history. This museum, full of information about the history of mining in Colorado, was right up his alley.

"Oh, so you meant a *nerdy* old geezer," Sadie said, and Alfred threw back his head and let out a belly laugh. Alfred and his wife, Cecile, had long been friends of Sadie and her late husband T.R., and Alfred and Roz had crossed paths many times through the years, so it made Sadie glad to see them joking around together.

"I think you'll find plenty of history to devour in the exhibit Sadie has put together for the Silver Festival," Karen Langdon, the museum's director, said, gesturing for them all to move on through into the special exhibits room. Karen was tall and thin, with short blonde hair and a deep tan that belied the hours she spent inside keeping this museum running. Like Sadie, Karen often got invited to events put on by the town government since her husband, Clark, was on the city council. "The display is really quite impressive, Sadie, especially considering how little time you had to pull it together."

Sadie felt her cheeks flush. "I love bringing history to life," she said. "If it gets people interested in the past, then it's all worth it."

The Silver Festival was an annual event that celebrated the history of Colorado silver mining, which for many years had been the primary industry in this area.

Though the festival was hosted by the museum, it was always organized entirely by volunteers from the community. This year, Sadie had been asked to take over as festival director just a couple weeks ago, after Jeanne Sweeting, who had organized the festival for the past few years, had had surgery on her knee after a bad fall. Jeanne was outgoing and loved planning events, but she had to concede that she wouldn't be able to pull it all together on crutches. Since Sadie loved sharing the fascinating past of her hometown, she had agreed to give organizing the event a shot, though she felt unprepared for the scope of the task. The exhibit she was putting together at the museum was the centerpiece of the festival, with the valuable Riley silver as the main attraction.

The three antique silver pieces—a simply worked but starkly beautiful bowl, platter, and cup—at the heart of the exhibit had been made from the first batch of silver ore pulled from the Riley mine, and as such they were both incredibly old and extremely valuable. Now they were being publicly displayed for the first time ever.

"I'm just glad you weren't scared away by the rumors about the curse," Karen said. "You'd be surprised how many people through the years have said no to the task because of it."

"What curse?" Alfred looked up from the display of tools in the glass case by the door.

"It's a silly old legend," Aiden said, gesturing for Alfred to step through the doorway. He'd only been on the job for a few weeks, but Sadie was impressed by the amount of local information he'd soaked up in that time. "You've heard about all the disasters at the Riley Mines through the years?"

Alfred nodded. Everyone—well, everyone who cared about Rocky Mountain history, anyway—had heard about the series of unfortunate cave-ins and unexplained explosions in the Riley Company's silver mines. Through the years, dozens of men had died underground in its tunnels.

"Well, people say that the Silver Festival is a legacy of that, and that the role of director is cursed because of it," Aiden said, shaking his head. A history major at Colorado Mountain College, Aiden had shown himself to be methodical and rational in recent weeks, and Sadie wasn't surprised to see he didn't believe in the old rumors. "Of course it's not true, but..."

"There are a lot of people around here who would disagree with you there," Roz said, stepping toward the doorway. "Jeanne is only the latest director to fall victim to the curse. Don't forget about Roger Scholl, who fell right into a patch of poison ivy right after he ran it a few years ago. And there's Grace Adley, whose cat got in that unfortunate fight with the skunk just before the festival a while back."

Sadie shook her head. Roz was listing a series of unfortunate events to befall festival directors, but surely she could see that they were just coincidences. There was no reason to assume they had anything to do with this ridiculous curse.

"And then there's the most famous one," Karen said, wiping a smudge off the edge of a glass case with her sleeve as she walked past.

"David Phillips," Roz said simply. Sadie could see that it still bothered Roz to think about it. Her husband Roscoe had been very friendly with David, and Roz had gotten to know him as well.

Albert raised an eyebrow.

"He was the director what, twenty years ago now?" Karen said, and Roz nodded. They had stopped moving and were gathered in a small clump by the doorway to the special exhibit gallery. "He put on a fantastic festival, and then drove away at the end of the day and never made it home. He was never seen or heard from again. They never found out what happened to him."

Even though Sadie thought their line of reasoning was silly, she still had to cringe at the reminder of that sad story. David had been a pillar in the community—a doctor who loved restoring antique cars and volunteering as an usher at the opera—and then, just like that, he'd vanished. They never found any trace of him.

"That's horrible, but it's hardly proof of a curse," Aiden said, flashing a smile at Sadie to show that he was on her side. She met his eyes and smiled back.

Roz shrugged. "Well, maybe it was, and maybe wasn't. But you can't deny there's a long list of misfortunes that have befallen those poor people crazy enough to take on the role." She flashed a smile at her friend. "No offense, Sadie."

"None taken," Sadie said. "Especially because, like Aiden, I think it's all nonsense." Sadie could agree that a series of sad events had sidelined a number of the previous festival directors, but no doubt there had been plenty of good things that had happened as well. "Which is why I think this year's festival is going to be the best yet."

Sadie stepped into the room where she'd designed and set up special displays about the history of the Riley Company's mines. For decades, the Riley Company had been one the largest producers of silver ore in the region, and her exhibition featured a special display of some of its founder's journals and letters. She called back into the other room, where the others were still lingering, "The Riley Silver is the centerpiece of the exhibit, as you'll see when you follow me inside."

"Subtle," Roz said, and finally walked through the doorway into the Special Exhibits gallery. Alfred walked in behind her, followed closely by Aiden, and Karen Langdon brought up the rear.

"So where is this famous silver that's caused so much trouble?" Roz looked around the main area of the gallery, and took in the journals and letter in glass cases and historical photos of the prosperous mine mounted on foam board.

"It's in the next room," Sadie said, indicating a smaller room off the main space. "In this area, you'll be able to read

Bartholomew Riley's papers." The Riley Mines had been closed for decades, but Bartholomew Riley loomed large in the history of Silver Peak, and viewing his personal effects helped humanize and bring to life this man who had played such an important role in their town—and whose wealth, gleaned from the ore in the hills that surrounded the small city—had funded so much of the city's growth. "You'll learn about how he bought the land in 1875 without knowing there was any silver underground, and how everything changed when the ore was discovered in 1879."

Sadie gestured toward the grainy black-and-white photos of men with pick-axes posed in front of the mouth of the mine. Next to them hung the paragraphs she'd written about how the discovery of silver had led to the influx of prospectors hoping to stake their claims and strike it rich. Those men and women had settled the town that became known as Silver Peak. "And here"—she gestured to a blank spot on the wall—"is where I intend to hang information about the mines today, and some information about mining around…"

"Yeah, yeah," Roz said, waving her words away. Bangles on her wrist smacked together, and a smile lit up her face. "We all know about all that. We're here to see that silver." She started toward the door on the far side of the room, and Sadie laughed and started to follow after her.

"Yeah, let's see this display so I can assure Pete it's safe. You can never trust places like this," Alfred laughed.

She smiled. She couldn't be offended by her friends' light-hearted ribbing. The pieces were owned by Pete Redell, a friend of Albert's who lived in Breckenridge, and had never been displayed at the museum before. Sadie's having secured them for the Silver Festival had been considered something of a coup, and because

Pete couldn't make it down himself to see and approve the display, he'd asked Alfred to come check it out and verify that they were secure before the festival began. The museum was closed today, as it was every Monday, but this was the only day Alfred Daly could make it down to Silver Peak, so Sadie has arranged this special tour for this morning. Aiden had put a lot of work into the display and was anxious to show his uncle what he'd been up to, and Karen, as the museum director, was here to supervise. Roz had been helping Sadie with some of the details of the festival, and technically she was here to see the pieces so she could help answer questions about them on Saturday, but if Sadie didn't know better she'd think Roz had come mostly to heckle.

"All right, all right. The silver pieces are right through here," Sadie said, walking backward through the archway into the smaller room. "The pieces had gotten fairly tarnished after being in the bank vault for so long, so we polished them. They should stay shiny through the festival at least, especially because the air in this museum…"

Sadie stopped mid-sentence when she saw the stricken looks on the faces of the people following her into the room.

"Where is…," Karen said, her voice faltering.

Sadie whipped around, and her heart dropped when she took in what the others had already seen.

No. No, it couldn't be.

"There has to be a mistake," Sadie said, looking around the room for answers. All she saw were blank faces, staring back at her.

"Sadie, isn't it supposed to be…," Alfred started, and Sadie nodded. The silver was supposed to be right there on the pedestal. But it wasn't. And she had no idea what had happened to it.

A Note from the Editors

WE HOPE YOU ENJOYED *MYSTERIES OF SILVER PEAK*, PUBLISHED BY the Books and Inspirational Media Division of Guideposts, a nonprofit organization that touches millions of lives every day through products and services that inspire, encourage, help you grow in your faith, and celebrate God's love.

Thank you for making a difference with your purchase of this book, which helps fund our many outreach programs to military personnel, prisons, hospitals, nursing homes, and educational institutions.

We also create many useful and uplifting online resources. Visit Guideposts.org to read true stories of hope and inspiration, access OurPrayer network, sign up for free newsletters, download free e-books, join our Facebook community, and follow our stimulating blogs.

To learn about other Guideposts publications, including the best-selling devotional *Daily Guideposts*, go to Guideposts.org/Shop, call (800) 932-2145, or write to Guideposts, PO Box 5815, Harlan, Iowa 51593.

Sign up for the
Guideposts Fiction Newsletter
and stay up-to-date on the books you love!

You'll get sneak peeks of new releases, recommendations from other Guideposts readers, and special offers just for you . . .

and it's FREE!

Just go to Guideposts.org/Newsletters today to sign up.

Guideposts.

**Visit Guideposts.org/Shop
or call (800) 932-2145**